The Bed and Breakfast Chronicles

The Bed and Breakfast Chronicles

David Dom-Estos

Illustrators:

Stephen Patrick Hanna, &

Kayleigh A.Wilson-Reyes.

This book was printed in the United States of America.

CONTENTS

Acknowledgements

Many thanks for their patience with the many alterations and adjustments they had to make in the production of imagery, Our 2 young student artists stayed at the B&B over a weekend to get to know the place and some of the routines associated with running a business. They had been given there own separate area to spread out and work with the many images that were required. They knuckled down and produced all 40 or so images within a 2 week window. This was a lot of work to get through as well as studying full time at Uni. Well done both of you and thanks again.

Introduction

This book has been based on the memories of happenings associated with the day to day running of our 2 Bed and Breakfast's. The first B&B,(1) started 7 years ago and the second B&B,(2) some 3 years later. The two run separately but are linked as the author and fiancée have a close partnership. We jointly have regular guests staying and as written some move between 1 & 2.

Our experiences have us talking at great length to ascertain if any credibility can be reasoned to the antics of some guests.

I have only found out since running the B&B that people are the strangest beings on the planet. They say animals and children are un-predictable but adults take the biscuit!

I have lived and worked with loads of people with similar views, aims and values as myself but when that complete stranger comes through your door just wait and see another world unfold, his world.

It has been fascinating as we do not know what is going to happen tomorrow.

I hope we can keep going for a few more years and try to note any out of the ordinary or memorable occurrences so I can pen them in The B&B chronicles 2.

You might have to wait a bit?

Author; David Dom-Estos

A new start after 35 years of appeasing
Customer's in my building business.

Chapter 1

First days

I was thinking that if I could no longer do my building work I would have to find another source of income. I spoke to my wife about this and said how easy it would be to run a bed and breakfast from home. We now had a 5/6 bedroom bungalow, extended as the children grew up, and it would be ideal to convert.

Well it happened around my 55th birthday. I had to give up my building work on medical grounds and decided at that time to start the B&B. This took some time to get going as the rooms were family rooms and were not en-suite. This I thought would be ok so rack-em, stack-em and pack-em . . . in, was the thought. I bought bed and mattresses and piled in as many as I could. I wanted bums on beds, the more the merrier. This was not going to be a high class B&B, just clean and convenient.

The first 2 guests I had got right up my nose. They were smokers.

The signs clearly state 'NO SMOKING' however smoke must have got in their eyes. They only stayed the one night. After a large 'Full Monty' breakfast they were gone saying what a lovely place I had here and would definitely be coming back, yeah . . . right!

Their room was number 4, a triple on the first floor. Immediately I noticed the smell of stale smoke infesting the room. An attempt to mask this with the bedroom window fully open in mid-winter didn't do it! Outside the window I found 20 or so fag butts thrown into the rain gutter. I thought how am I gonna get them out of there then?

I started stripping the beds with my nose being assaulted with this filthy odour. It was horrible and I started working at full speed to remove all the affected materials.

What was this I was experiencing? I was used to being down smelly stinky sewers in my previous occupation? Was this a mental thing? Was I expecting the room to smell as it did before these blokes arrived? The new carpet was my main concern, as this would not go in the washing machine . . . what to do? Well years ago I had heard mother say, 'I'll do the shake and vac'. I thought this was some rock music exercise regime when she did the house work. So anyway, off to the local shop to get some stuff.

I wondered if this was part of the reason why my young wife (18 years married), divorced me, saying that she was not going to be a landlady at the age of 35.

Returning with the necessary gear I sprayed, vacuumed, washed and perfumed the room but the smell still lingered, or was it just my imagination?

That night with the beds neatly made up, the window firmly shut, the radiator nice and hot the next guests arrived. They signed in and paid for 2 nights with full English breakfast, requesting to be served at 9 am. Quick and neat then! Taking them up the stairs, I asked them to lower their heads on the low beam about half way up. I reminded them to 'limbo' down in the morning. Just in case, I pointed to the sign right above the beam stating, OUCH too late! You should have lowered your head?"

With un-ease I opened the door and to my surprise the room was pleasantly fresh, what was my problem then? This B&B lark was not all that bad!

I retired for the night and didn't hear them come in from a late dinner at the pub/restaurant over the road. The next morning brought the 2 men down. One had a plaster on his head and I said, "Was that going up last night?" He said, "I forgot!"

I said, "Would you like to go through to the dining room?" The table was laid out for 6 guests, with place mats, cups, glasses, condiments, sugar bowl, all newly-filled. Table napkins were jauntily placed inside the individual glasses. "This is very nice", one said. I thanked him and requested their order, which

I could tell was, 'The Full Monty'. Bacon, eggs, beans, tomatoes, mushrooms, toast, tea/coffee, juice and preserves, gut-bustin!

With all that finished, I washed up and put away and re-laid the table for the next morning. Just then they came back down and left for their 1st days training, starting at 9.45am. This was the reason they were stopping here for 2 days in mid winter. They arrived back at tea time. I offered them a refreshing cuppa. They both had headaches with the sudden influx of information they had absorb that day. They looked tired so after drinking the tea they went upstairs to get ready to go out for an early dinner. On the way down the second guy developed more of a headache as he also forgot the low beam.

I could get used to the little dull thump on the staircase. They returned from dinner and all went quiet for the night. The next morning breakfast went as the first and they left saying that I had a very nice place here and we both had a very comfortable stay.

'This B&B lark isn't all that bad', I said to myself . . .

Chapter 2

First days, continued.

I was running the show alone but the B&B brought me a steady flow of company. My mind went back 12 years when we, as a family, had a ginger tom called Hobie. I had a sailing catamaran called a Hobie-cat at the time so I named him after it . . . Hobie. He was about a year old and was run over in the road just outside our place. Our Daughter aged 5 brought tears to my saddened eyes when in his burial box she wanted Hobie to have her cherished silky bedtime doll. The doll that she stoutly refused to let anybody take away from her, even to wash it.

So then, for company I thought it's time I brought home another cat, a kitten, this time a pure white male I called Mr Socket. I know this sounds silly but when you saw the three black spots on his forehead in the shape of a triangle Socket seemed appropriate, especially to a—builder/plumber/electrician.

New guests arrived and there was the mum and dad with the little girl. They were in the downstairs family room with the double bed and a single bed alongside. The outlook was to the garden and at just below sill level was the fish pond adjoined to the house, on the outside wall. Any children staying in this room loved to stand on the bed and look out at the 40 or so fish waiting for their breakfasts. They were shown into the dining room, with the parents wanting the full Monty, and the child having my special scrambled egg, spread over buttered toast, crusts removed and with the smiley face run in tomato ketchup around the plate. All was going well when I found the family had migrated to the lounge and looking out over towards the fish pond alongside the lounge window. A howl of excitement erupted and on investigating I found Socket with the child's banana-yellow knitted doll firmly 'killed' in his mouth. He had snuck in and dragged it from their bedroom to the lounge, trailing it between bandy legs. Safe under a dining chair, in full view of the family Socket started to shake and claw the doll in an absolute frenzy.

I was horrified as I know how passionate little girls feel about their dolls, special dolls. To my amazement the family took out a camera phone and started to record the event with the little girl laughing with all. Socket was a character and endeared himself with these people unlike the next guest.

She came to stay a few days, a college course, on art at the nearby Uni. She showed me her work from a portfolio she had produced. Some of the images were dramatic and had a real lifelike presence, very-good indeed.

She was a beautiful young lady that made me wish I was young again to stand any chance of chatting her up. Her skin tone was of mixed race, possibly Asian / English, with model facial features and neat body.

I put her in the family room which has multi-colourful large spot bedding, a compliment to the rather staid plain magnolia walls and dark green carpet. The downstairs bathroom is adjacent to her room so she has to walk across a small hall between the 2 rooms to get to it. I have the room opposite and can hear the creaking floorboards when someone walks across the hall and in this case I thought if only!

I have had men guests, 'open' my bedroom door by mistake, half asleep and disorientated thinking they were entering 'their bedroom', never a young female. What a shock, what a disappointment, is this how B&B life is to be.

All seemed 'Tickity Boo' until Day 3 when she complained and showed me her legs. Under any other circumstances this would have been the progress I wanted but alas, No.

It was flea bites!

My mate Socket had snuck in her room and taken the little critters in with him. He had no doubt picked them up in my garden or more likely from his cat friends. I sometimes heard squealing as he chased any infiltrators through the kitchen cat flap. She wasn't happy and said she had to leave immediately. Well I had no chance with her anyway and Socket saw to it that he was my *only* partner for now, OK. Meeow!

Chapter 3

Using Socket to get a girl

Running the B&B, besides keeping my head above water, the women I accommodated could result in getting me a date. Every possible female guest was a candidate for this, but alas as yet, No joy. *Years before, in my previous single life I helped my brother in law for a while with his a milk round. Did any sexy lady ever come to the door in her night dress, not on your Nelly, Never?*

So how could I use Socket then? Well I looked through my picture folder and found by accident that Socket was sat next to me when I took a self portrait for the dating agency website?

"This was it!" I thought. Get this gorgeous cat to take the limelight and distract from my rather rugged features, aged 55 plus, and woo the girls' hearts by having a cat, 'caring nature'. Another plan was to use a stage name to catch the attention of the babes. I thought of Richard Gere and said I was his Brother David Gere. By accident my photo looked somewhat like Richard's especially viewed from the side and rear, so much so that against the rules of the dating site I posted one of his pictures along side mine and said "Richard or me?"

Well—success—as after a couple of weeks I had 1235 viewings of my profile with just 4 wanting more info. You can't fool the babes for long . . . just appeal to their curiosity. Well of the four, two wore cardigans and the other two were older than me, doh!

My daughter was now 17. She said that her friend thought I looked a bit like Richard Gere but now that my hair has grown a bit she reckons I look more like Mrs Doubtfire. I did in desperation want to try out these 2 older women but I thought travelling a long way at the weekends is a non-starter for my B&B business you know! So back to the drawing board then!

I dwelled on the viewings for about 3 months and decided another strategy; this was to get them to visit me, free of charge at the B&B, offering them their own room, in perfect safety. Nothing! Not even cardigan girls took up the challenge.

The trouble with me is I still think I'm 21, until one day I did try and date one older woman. To my surprise she was good company talked my language, went to bed early, as tired as I was. She didn't mind all my silly jokes, made food without a fuss . . . but she was not for me. I wanted nice but naughty? I still had some boyish spirit to vent.

There was this German girl who booked for a month. She was a lot younger than me but a mature student. I forget her name, but after a couple weeks or so she asked if her girl friend visiting from Germany could stay in her room . . . for free? Well I was not having it? Everyone pays. I said she could have it cheaper than the going rate, with no breakfast. Her friend reluctantly agreed and paid for a week. After her friend went back home German girl's Uni course ran on for another 10 days. She looked so sad and alone. I thought I would cheer her up one evening and asked if she would like to come and be with me one night. She came down to my lounge, sitting beside me on the double settee. We watched TV and had some drinks. 'I might be ok here' I thought so after some more small talk I made my move. I was stopped short as I was told she was 'faithful', to her . . . girlfriend! Oopps!

Not this time or any with her it seems? It was late by now and she returned or retreated to her room.

Making so many early breakfasts I thought it would be easier to let out the upstairs on self catering basis. This is when a Spanish teacher came to stay, teaching French at a local school to children who didn't want to learn English. I got to drinking with him on occasion and found he was in the same boat as me, single and handsome . . . Ha, ha. He was here for a year and a half but again this dual habitation problem came up as he quickly found a Romanian girlfriend. The first week I saw her she was a blonde then later a brunette. I went up to see them and found, drizzled over the cream carpet, black dye from her hair, well nightmare.

I had to replace the carpet saying, "please be careful as this piece was the last replacement bit I had." They stayed for about a year together and when they left she was, red haired. Yes, you guessed, the carpet was drizzled with red dye. On top of that the walls were peppered with blue tack and the wooden beams had about 40 screwed in rings for hanging items up. The carpet was grey, the new fridge had broken plastic trays and, well, the whole place had to have a refit and repaint.

That didn't work out money wise so it's back to Bed & Breakfast for the upstairs then!

Chapter 4

The first holiday break

It was late summer and I had to have a break so I chose a 4 day caravan break. The van I borrowed free of charge from my ex brother-in-law. Remember the milk round? Well, this old van was a little 2 berth with the usual facilities. Bringing along our 2 boys meant them camping in a tent outside the van. The site was close to my B&B just in case of emergencies.

This was an exploratory event as I was taking, for the first time since my divorce, a female away with her son, who was best friends with my son. Our original meeting was arranged by the 2 boys. His mother was going to be at their school so if I picked up my son this particular afternoon, we could 'accidently meet each other'. Well a tall woman of 40-something came over and chatted to me while I was waiting in my car. She knew it was me as the boys had given her my car description, make and colour. I liked her and I thought I was doing well so I asked her out, trying not to sound too desperate. We met again later that evening, (that quick) and went for a drink up the local pub. We started seeing each other from then on. A success at last! Well done boys!

I thought it would be a good idea if I planted a rose in my garden at the B&B to remind me of her. I chose a lovely pink, sweet smelling climbing rose that seemed to suit her look—tall and sweet, pink lipstick.

We got to the campsite early evening and the boys set up their tent. We had a barbeque kit so on the first night all we did was to spoil some good food on the contraption. It was fun and after a few drinks we turned in. In the morning we found the place didn't have a swimming pool, but just up the road, free to use at their sister site, they had. Our site had nothing but a pub/bar sort of thing with heated snacks only. The other star features were a bank of 3 washing machines. A pay-to-use system was in force but they were never free, always full of washing, so I didn't get to use them. Oh! A hole for waste, I forgot that, well I wouldn't know how to use that anyhow. Tell me the attraction for caravanning again? We went out to various fun places: skiing on a dry slope, getting drunk, having a meal out, that sort of thing.

The days went quickly and then the inevitable call came. My workman was staying at my place, temporarily, while building a replacement wall in the front. This building work was overdue as one of my ex-wife's friends had driven her car smack-bang into one of the piers on an earlier visit. Woman drivers? It wasn't a small entrance either as I already widened it for my big truck and trailer to reverse into easier.

My workman was asked to feed the cat and birds and make sure they had water. Both my birds, he said, had died overnight. They were a loved cockatoo and a male budgie who thought was his mate. They were happy together. Arriving home I found the budgie outside the cage with some twine around its neck lying dead in the food tray on the floor and the cockatoo lying cold on the cage floor. Was this an anguished death from the demise of the budgie? It was a sad ending to a rather poor holiday attempt. Caravanning, you can keep it.

I had the task of returning the van to my ex brother-in-law. We didn't use any of the van's cooking facilities but kept some food for sandwiches in the fridge. So after dropping it back, parking it nicely on their drive, in the same place it was a few days earlier, I left thanking them very much. It was great! A week later they phoned and said what a disgusting mess we had left the van in and requested I come over to see it. I was gobsmacked and amazed at this and went over straight away. It smelt like a throng of unwashed labourers had dost in there for a month. On inspection it was found that the carpet was wringing wet through as the fridge had defrosted in the week and the contaminated water made the carpet smell so bad that it had to be replaced.

To make things worse this carpet had only been fitted days before we borrowed it, second-hand but newly fitted. "It was not my fault!" I argued. The drain-off for the fridge was blocked and the smelly frozen water was absorbed into the old/new carpet. "Not my fault", I uttered. She said, well it was because if we had not let you use it you would have not put the fridge on so it would have not overflowed. Some logic I thought but what about when you use the fridge? "Are you going to keep it running for ever, I asked?" "That would be our problem then" she said. She was not happy, I was not happy, everybody was not happy.

This was my experience of my first holiday caravanning whilst running a B&B. I will think twice about borrowing another caravan. I will think twice about leaving all my stuff for others to look after.

Just one other thing, when on the camp site, the boys were sent off up the road to the swimming pool which that left us 2 'young lovers' alone for a while. With the van door locked and the window open a little for air, we got down to some private Tiffin? Half way through this delight the boys poked their heads through the open window just above the bed and one said, "Hello Dad! Have you got any money for drinks?" No, not on me!

Chapter 5

The dying man

Up until now I have not killed anyone for eating my breakfasts but this time I was accused of feeding her husband with the wrong food.

I had a locum, a dispensing chemist staying for 2 months. It was colder now, November 2nd and the only other resident I had was a Spaniard living alone in the flat, who was already starting to bleat about the cold. He had only been here for a few weeks since the September school term started.

Anyhow this chemist was from another country as well. It reminds me of a schoolboy joke. *Where do women have the curliest hair? I can see into your mind and that's not right? It's not what you're thinking! Its . . . . Africa.*

Ok He came from South Africa. He was a big man over 6 foot and always got up at 7 am, came down at 7.30, had the full Monty including my special beans and toddled off to work which was a half-hour walk away He arrived back home always after 9 pm so presumably he left work walked back and had dinner at the local pub. I didn't inquire as, like clockwork, this carried on for a month and only altered on Sundays. He didn't speak more than a half a dozen times in general conversation so I didn't know to much about his background.

He came to the foot of the stairs looking dead grey. Well I hadn't ever seen someone looking grey before but it came to me he was having a heart attack. I told him to stay there and I went up to his room and collected his big black overcoat. I said I was going to take him directly to the local hospital where he would be taken care of and everything was going to be alright. I went up to the flat quickly and got the *shivering* Spaniard to come and drive us to the hospital. We started coaxing him slowly into the front seat of the car, conscious of his laboured breathing and heavy wheezing.

The Spaniard's car was a little on the small side for us let alone this big guy. Anyhow we wedged him in and arrived at the hospital in good time. He obviously couldn't walk so we had to scramble and find a wheelchair. Would you believe it, they were chained up with a coin operated release. I found a pound coin and unlocked the chair. *Just imagine not getting to the crash team because we didn't have a pound coin.* I didn't realise that hospitals are like supermarkets . . . well maybe they are?

Our job done! He was whisked away into the bowels of the A&E department as we waited at the reception desk to give his and our details. With nothing else to do we left and went for a quick drink up the pub. It's amazing when your adrenalin is up how you deplete nervous energy without realising it. I needed the drink. Later I waited at home for some good news. The Spaniard said he thought he heard two loud thumps on the floor earlier in the evening, like someone had fallen down. He was right cos when I went upstairs to check lights etc there was a string of bright red blood spots running over the hot sand carpet leading from his bed to the bathroom. I don't have much luck with droppings on this carpet do I? It was 10.30 pm now and I was still awake with this situation, what if he died? What if it was my fault? What if? Then the phone rang and the news. He had died. Hell!

They could do nothing as he had been abusing himself for years. He was on insulin but he kept none in my fridge. I suspected he took it at work. He didn't as when I cleared up his room I found bottles in the wardrobe, just left there. The people he worked for said that he was slow, and every day he was getting slower and slower. They suspected he had a small heart attack just as he started his first day at work! Anyway the poor chap was earning for his wife back home and I suspect she was driving him hard. His money was considerable as I know from a previous locum. They get £24 per hour on holidays and Sundays. And some work lots of hours even at the standard rate I worked out they get up to £700 per week.

This man was a work horse and when the wife phoned the next morning she was a 'Rottweiler'. She had no regard for him just to say, "What did you feed him for this to happen?" Well I ask you, no inquiry about, "did he say anything about me" or "was he ok generally", "was he happy?" Nope, just "pack up his bags and things and I will get his cousin from Colchester to pick them up". An endearing woman! Well she had just lost her excellent income and what was she gonna do now? Collect on his will I suspect.

Colchester arrived and gave me his identification and we opened Locum's suitcase, which was locked. Chopping off the little padlocks Colchester found his cheque book as I wanted this week's money £140.

I know that sounded bad taking money from a dead man but I didn't want her to have it, after all I had to totally revamp the room, new bed, carpet and repaint. I even repositioned the wardrobe. He was supposed to stay another month but this did give me time to organise his room.

Poor bloke I hardly knew him.

Chapter 6

My manhood comes into question . . .

It was on this morning that 2 young couples came for the night. In the morning all 4 wanted breakfast so I sat them in the dining room. I had on my new pink 'Hackett' pure wool jumper and a striped kitchen apron to keep it splash free. This was one of my designer tops that I bought from TK Maxx. I thought I'd be a little smarter this morning as I was catering for the ladies. Well they were all very affable and chatty during the serving and I asked if the food was up to scratch. They all agreed that it was lovely and how did I do it all by myself. Well self-taught and by trial and error I said. After clearing away the plates they went to their rooms as I prepared to wash up. During my time at the sink one chap said he didn't know how I could do all this housework and gave me a strange look. Remembering I was wearing my pink Hackett I quickly replied in a deep voice well I've had a lot of years on building sites. I got divorced and thought I would try this B&B lark alone, as a complete lifestyle change. This has been a big learning curve for me. With that he seemed satisfied that my gender was intact. I added that I would never use marigold gloves even in the hottest water. Didn't need to say that did I?

After they left I realised that I had to overcome the male taboo that 'women's work' should be left to the women. Slowly in time this drifted away and now it seems that role reversal is accepted.

I have washed my Hackett a few times and make sure I keep it for going out, however when I put it on recently I thought that it was a bit tight around the belly as well as being very snug on the shoulders. I must have been working out without realising it, I thought, but no. I had washed it with the bed linen, on hot and my soft wool designer jumper had shrunk down to a tight knit. It would fit my son's smaller frame though. Would he take it over, it's hardly worn? He said, absolutely NOT. I wondered why?

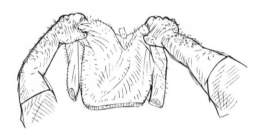

It's Saturday tomorrow and I am expecting 2 separate groups. 8 girls will occupy the flat and a group of 5 boys, all wanting single beds deployed elsewhere. Well the triple room upstairs and the family room next to me were available so I put 3 of the boys in the triple and the other 2 outside in the chalet.(*I didn't want them in the room next to me).* The chalet has 2 bunks and heating. TV, carpets, but no facilities, so they will have to come indoors to shower etc.

The trouble started when the whole group congregated on the front car park waiting for the 4 taxis I had ordered for them. The boys now knew that 8 young girls, dressed to kill were staying inches away from them tonight. They thought their lottery ticket had come up. The taxis arrived and I went to bed at 10.45 pm.

The phone woke me at 3.30 am with a harassed and worried little voice calling, 'please come and tell the boys to stop tapping the windows, their frightening us'? I went outside and found 2 up on the balcony making themselves a nuisance, and the other 3 smoking and playing music from a small transistor perched on the garden table. I yelled, "You 2, come down at once? All you lot have to go party elsewhere. You come here to sleep not to party so either go back to town or go to bed". I was very cross being woken at this time in the morning. Well, all went quiet and the rest of the night was uneventful.

The morning brought the tired revellers up at about 11am. The boys were smiling and in good humour, but the girls were not so happy. The boys left saying they would like to come back sometime soon as the place was 'fab'. The girls said the episode left them scared and would not be back again. My dilemma is I would like the girls back and not the boys? I can't win!

Going up to the flat where the girls stayed I changed my mind. Make-up everywhere and no toilet paper left. What can 8 girls do with 3 rolls of toilet paper in one night? They used the sheets to wipe their faces off as it seemed all the toilet paper was gone. The sheets and pillows were covered with black mascara, pink and red lipstick, glitter everywhere. The lounge had 35 various empty bottles and drinks containers arranged neatly on the table for me to clear. I went to the under cupboard waste bin only to find it filled with . . . more bottles, rude cocktail straws and paper umbrellas, what a night we all had.

Thankfully no damage was done and the sheets came clean, so my first big 'dual sex' occupancy was over. Perhaps I would take the boy's back as they weren't that bad, after all it wasn't them who phoned to wake me up at 3.30am. I can't win!

Chapter 7

What curve comes next?

Time for a holiday. I arranged to take my kids to Tenerife for a week's holiday and all went well. The weather was great and the time in the sun was just what I needed. This time I was incommunicado so nothing was going to spoil my relaxation. I still have the caricature hanging up on my kitchen wall. Refreshed now we returned to meet a rather messy house. There had been an incident, and the house sitter, an employee of mine who was about to retire, was left in charge. He was gone and I shuddered to think what I was going to find. Well I looked all around only to see in my bedroom the wardrobe had been ransacked and on inspection found the safe had been removed from the wall. I immediately rang the police and when they arrived we started to analyse the situation. I went to the garage and found my grinding tools left everywhere and some belongings of the employee, a lighter, damaged glasses, other tools of his etc. The police drove me to his flat some miles away to find nothing. Asking next door if they had seen him, but no. This was planned as he asked me before I went away if I had received the balance of cash from our last job. I said I was going to pick it up on Saturday just before the bank holiday weekend. As I was flying out early Tuesday he knew that the money was going to be in my safe.

That gave him all week to crack it and get away with the cash. I never gave this a thought as he was not the only person in the house.

I found out later he had been grinding for hours in the garage but the neighbours didn't suspect anything as this type of activity was normal for us builders. 3 days it took him to grind a bit at a time through the hardened safe to get at his loot. The cheeky bugger even bought on my account at the local builder's merchants, more grinding discs to finish the job. He didn't even try to cover up his actions as he left a hand written note saying, 'Sorry', 'better me than the vat or taxman'. *He couldn't even spell the word Sorry.* Nice of him to apologise though!

A year or so later he was caught sleeping rough in his car by the road in a remote part of Scotland and was remanded in custody. At his trial he said he gave half of the money to charity, and said he spent the rest. He had another conviction from a previous incident in like circumstances where he had gained the trust of his victim. He worked self employed for me, unattended in my customer's homes for 7 years with no incident. His credentials included one of his own customers, his friend and sergeant at the local police station, with whom he attended church regularly. I was shocked as was everyone who knew him over this 7 year period. Who do you trust? He was convicted and sent to jail for 14 months.

This was no justice for me or the other victims as well as all who knew him. We all felt let down by a minimal jail sentence and betrayed by this sad and cunning individual hiding within the Christian community.

I also gave him a loan of £1000 as deposit for the flat previously mentioned and along with this and the total amount of cash in the safe his short lived joy amounted to £ 21,000.00.

A point of interest was that my cleaning lady came on Wednesdays and he would not let her into my bedroom to clean. I didn't leave her £20 for her cleaning fee so she wanted to get it from my safe. She threatened to phone me for the combination. Well it turned out he didn't want that so he gave her £20 out of his pocket to keep her away from the safe. He had already tampered with it and the electronics locked out the keyboard. If she saw this she would have known he had been trying to open it by guessing the combination. If she had rung me in Tenerife then he might have been thwarted there and then . . . If only!

After a restless night's sleep I started to pick up the pieces and wondered what will come next time I have a holiday. I can't blame these things on holidays so it must be who I leave in charge. I have to plan in future to completely close down for the duration.

Soon the customers start phoning for beds, my routine has started again and I have to get my gardener to trim the leylandii. He arrives demanding tea and with his Romanian labourer (oh no!) He starts hacking. There are about 50 trees to do and some are very close to my lounge wall. After a trailer full of branches they leave clutching £100 in cash. The work was neat and all finished so in the evening I could relax, switch on the tele for the news and what this? No signal. Yup he has cut the Sky satellite cable. Outside I go, get a ladder, clamber up to the roof and make the repair.

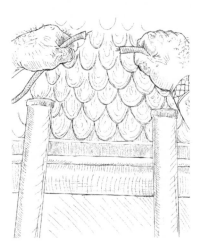

Lucky I had a co-axial joiner in the toolbox. I had to do it quick as all the TVs in the house went out and the guests were moaning straight away. The telly's gone off? That bloody gardener will be in for it tomorrow.

Chapter 8

Another attempt at internet dating . . .

I thought that I would try again at internet dating and this time I posted my profile on 3 sites. I meant business this time. The picture I posted was one that my daughter took whilst on holiday. I had my arm around the 'ex-girlfriend' (pink rose) so her bit was cut off and only showed just my head and shoulders. It didn't look half bad as I had a rosy (pun) glow with all that sun. My relationship with the girlfriend was going nowhere as she said that she had, 'unfinished business with a former boyfriend', well that was that then I suppose.

I was still feeling a little upset over failing in my marriage but life must go on and I learnt years before that it's no good dwelling on what cannot be. I will always have my memories and I wanted to gather some more.

So this internet dating game was in full swing. I had 3 sites on the go and one brought up local females most of the time as I said, only 5 miles from my base. The other 2 sites were country wide and this gave a broader range of woman. I stated I wanted females aged 18 to 45, a big gap but you have to speculate, sugar daddies have fun, don't they? I tried a few locally but none seemed up to the ex-wife, they all had baggage and I was free of that just now. My idea was to fall for some young beauty that just wanted someone older that could care for them in return for a steadier more secure life. Well bring out the champagne and it was supplied by the dating site as a success story was reported. I saw in my mail box a lady, blonde, good looking and my age. Well hit me with a wet kipper, she had assets that looked good in pairs. The drawback was she lived 140 miles away. Oh hell. Couldn't miss this chance though, so diving in head first I contacted her. All was going ok and true to form I asked if she would mind driving the 140 miles to visit me, in the sunshine, for a little break, away from her routine. I mentioned the B&B and the usual attractions of that. Next thing she arrived on the doorstep looking not unlike her picture.

This was a refreshing change as most of them were not as pretty as depicted in their photos. A broad smile must have come over my face as she entered seemingly unruffled from her long car journey. It was a bit of a blur from then on as I cannot recall exactly what happened only that some months later after many visits down here and just a couple of me going in her direction, we popped the champagne cork sportingly supplied by you know who.

Knowing that this girl was the one, we decided that to be together in the same town seemed the best bet. When her job in London came to an end, due to retirement, this was the opportunity for her to sell up and come to live here. Some travel arrangements were made as stuff from her house had to be transported down the 140 miles. Whilst running the B&B this had to be done quickly so I asked one of my guests to help and with him we managed the move in one day, with an overnight stay in her stripped out house. The following morning we finished loading the van and trailer to the max and trundled back home, in convoy with her old car full of all the girlie things with barely enough room for her to see out.

This time she was staying here in the B&B for good, not just visiting, so my lounge which is an extension of the dining area was completely filled with her extra furniture and stuff. The guests said that it looked like we were running an auction saleroom. Mostly the guests were sympathetic. Some weren't.

I didn't expect the routine to change as I was the master in the kitchen and the cleaning lady was good enough, but she had different ideas. Trouble ahead I thought.

Immediately the change to a spotless house was to be maintained. No more, 'that will do' attitude, so the new broom was here. Paint this, clean that, and don't put that on the bed it's disgusting! I didn't see it was that bad but I must admit some areas could be improved. So this was it, bliss, togetherness, someone to share the work with me.

Chapter 9

The garden and the new B&B

She was a dab hand in the garden. Together we defined the edges, weeded and covered the borders with hydroscopic weed-suppressing material and brought the whole garden centre's stock of decorative bark. The specimen plants followed and the roses planted in honour of each girlfriend I had dated over the years after divorce, named appropriately, had to be removed, leaving just the one, the bright yellow one. This one had to be repositioned so it was in the sunshine and not in the dark dingy corner which was the only place left to fit another rose. The lawns were mowed with that stripe that only the British seem to lust over and I must admit it is a picture, neat and tidy. I was thinking we could charge viewing and open a tea and scone service from the garden chalet. I had a hanging wind chime which had two ceramic fish with sharp white partly grinning teeth, piranhas, one large and one small.

These I found in France one year when I went sailing with my mates. I thought they depicted my ex-wife and my daughter precisely so I couldn't resist and I strung these up in a branch of the eucalyptus tree. This I am pleased to say were overlooked by 'Yellow Rose'.

It was fantasy of course to want to open the garden to visitors. The chalet had been occupied by our B&B overspill guest and removals man for some time now. He was comfortable in there as he kept himself to himself. *He could be the head gardener?* He had a great view in the morning from his veranda, looking at all the lovely plants and manicured lawns as he looked out. I had my reservations about having someone staying in the garden shed but in the summer you have to make do. I had a lady so desperate to stay that she pitched her tent on the small lawn, next to the trickle of the waterfall. She slept there for 2 nights. I didn't like to think what the tame fox thought of it all. He had to walk past all this to get to his sleeping spot on a disused camper bed in the greenhouse. Such was the accommodation problem at the time of a political party conference, with the delegates taking all the hotel rooms.

Having got my garden sorted out Yellow Rose found a problem that her house money was not making enough interest so it was broached that this B&B lark was working for me why no make it work for her also. She had learned from living here how it works and so we looked out for another suitable property. Well there was one nearby and so it was purchased in December. The place was a family home and needed some alterations, a new kitchen extension and double glazing. The garden was a mess and the flora around the property was well overgrown, so much so that it was hidden from the road. Well almost on the day of completion I got the digger out. I promptly got to work on the outside, clearing out the bamboo hedge, all the trees and the Victorian concrete path. With the site cleared it was just the garage, a wood and asbestos thing with a lighting cable coming from the eaves, resting right up against the new kitchen extension. My on, who was keen to drive the digger, requested a go. I said he could only drive a digger wearing a pink jumper? He looked glum but I was joking. Well his brief was to pull the garage down. So with one grabbing downward blow from the digger bucket he ripped through the fragile asbestos roof. Then with reverse gear selected moved backwards away from the extension dragging the whole garage with him reducing it to a mass of twisted timber and rubbish in one or two seconds. It took hours of graft to sort out the hardcore from the other stuff as some materials were needed to build up the ground for the new car park. We were to have a bonfire. All the broken timber extracted from various places were collected and heaped into a giant mount well away from the house. I set light to it and we were just standing watching it burn. The winter cold was replaced with the heat from the fire and we were just standing, drinking wine and waiting for the jacket potatoes in foil to bake. The fire attracted others passing by so it ended up as quite a get together. A nice way to meet the new neighbours!

The grabber lorry came the next day and removed all 13 tons of rubbish generated by the digger leaving us with the clear plot.

Over the next 8 weeks all my spare time was involved in completely revamping the inside to accommodate the new B&B. Rooms were made in the roof and new shower rooms were created. Every wall was papered and painted, new carpet laid.

Now the weather had changed and the outside could be tackled. The new car park was laid out with brick edgings to the perimeter. 50 trees were planted and a picket fence and gate were installed. The rest of the garden was laid to lawn and the small existing summer house repositioned on its new concrete base. The previous owner's garden swing was kept for the guests use.

It only left the tarmac boys to turn up and the job was completed. The sign was the very last thing to do and Yellow Rose was trading.

The first guests arrived in March and the fun began. Bed and breakfast number 2 had arrived.

Chapter 10

Learning the rules!

These are the first days of Yellow Rose running her own' B&B. B&B number2 is born.

I have explained earlier that when I became one with my internet date. I planted a Yellow Rose in my garden to see if it would survive. I did this for any girlfriend I had at the time. I do this for posterity. I have a dog rose growing in my hedge? Don't ask.

I did the right thing by digging it deep and adding adequate fertiliser then making sure that the roots were kept out of the sun. Roses like this. Their roots cool. Yellow Rose is called thus, because of her Yellow hair. She was unaware of these plantings as she as yet, was not fully incorporated into my life. We were still working on it as one has to be as sure as possible, at my age! We got it together and she showed me her intentions were fully committed.

To show how committed she was, my garden was to be cleaned up. That is, borders cleared and edges defined. Some of my roses had been in for years, and walking past them I had memories of the ladies now gone from my life. It was obvious that these roses were now neglected. I mused one had been let to run amok; others had been surrounded by plants or shrubs and lost their glory. In general these had no more interest for me. If one lady reared her head into my life again I would at least prune her and give her dignity back. After all, these were exciting days of relationships. Most were now resigned to rust, leaf curl and one in particular has rampant black spot.

Yellow Rose found out about this joy I have and immediately demanded that she was transplanted into pole position, in full sunshine, outshining all the others. I readily obliged and all was serene in the garden. She actually wanted them all removed but I explained that she was the one I cared for most so she let them stay.

Now you know the background let's see what happened when we got her B&B 2 up and running.

I had an idea that she could do this although she had not embarked on skivvying for others except for her direct family. This was different as strange people were to be catered for and without previous knowledge of 'guests' needs she would have to play it by ear.

I can say that when I started I wanted to do the best for my guests and so I would bend over backwards to please them. I would run about and ask if everything was ok. In the room were kettles and trays of coffee, tea, sugar and milk ready for the travellers to sit and revive themselves from their tiring journeys.

Every time I asked them if there was anything they required they always asked for this and that, things not strictly on offer. Things like can we use your iron? Can we just wash out these jeans as they got muddy in the rain when the car broke down on the way here? Can we just get a better room as we don't like the street light coming through the curtains? Can we, can we?

Well she soon found out NOT to ask if everything is alright. First rule.

Yellow Rose got this quite quickly as I think she is not as laid back as me about things. She went a bit Rottweiler with them, and I had to reel her back a bit because even I shuddered to hear her abrupt No's! And how dare you ask in the first place!

Chapter 11

Everything is new

Yellow Rose was in full swing and the first month of trading was over. The bed linen had been washed a few times and she had new purpose-made under valances for the divan bases. These she seamed up herself, bought the yards of material and slowly made these up, one by one, for every bed in the house. This looked good with the corners neat and middle pleats for decoration. None of your shop-bought rubbish here then?

I was concerned that she was going over the top with all this new clobber for Bed and Breakfast. She charges a lot less than hotels, and her price is including breakfast.

Well I was now in direct competition with her and so we had to have our prices comparable or soon she would have all the business and me, with years of grinding them out only get the runt end of the available trade for my efforts We came to a compromise as she wanted to get as many lets as possible. Her prices were easily 'negotiated down' by the customers, if they just hinted that £30 including breakfast was a bit steep. She would buckle and give them an alternative lower price. She would say, 'Well I could do it for . . . Say £25 per night'?

I found out that sometimes she would let out her best room for £20. You can't get a flea pit or dog kennel for that price around here. So what's so bad about £30 per night? The rooms, the beds, the linen are all brand new, never used, not a spot of dirt anywhere, wall tiles immaculate, flat screen TVs. Luxury I call it. She had to learn this was folly? People will try to price you down when I know that the average allowance for B&B for workmen working away is £50 . . . This is to include dinner. As she won't do evening meals she feels she has to help them with this, so charging only £ 20 they have £30 left for food. One can get a slap-up dinner and wine for that?

She has now agreed that £30 per night is fair 'especially, for the one nighters! All that work, changing beds, cleaning the room up, it's a lot to do after the breakfast stuff has been taken care of. This day in and day out will get to you. She will not compromise on cleanliness though. Keeping up standards! Good for her.

Having sorted out her routine she looked at her garden. I had planted 50 trees and they were to grow up to a thick hedge that kept the road traffic noise to a minimum. This would take a while so she had to put up with the constant traffic 'hum' until well after 11 pm.

Yellow Rose wanted to have her own room, the largest on offer. She chose the front room with all the lovely built-in wardrobes. This would be suitable for her needs.

You know! loads of designer gear collected over the years and only worn on that single special occasion. These clothes had to be saved for that single special occasion. If ever it came up, and so the big front room was chosen. It only lasted a week as the room with 4 windows on 2 sides brought masses of light in but the traffic noise was apparent in the background. Yellow Rose is a light sleeper and she said she didn't like the constant humming when she is lying in bed. Humming sound? Lying in bed? I shake my head at the thought of it! Not suitable then! I got it in the neck through her sleep deprivation.

We had to move all her stuff into the back room which would have been my choice as this was nearer the kitchen and directly opposite the loo. This room was further away from the road and proved most successful, for a while.

The guests kept drifting to her place. The managing director—and his girlfriend—from a firm of tiling contractors I had stay with me for a year, booked with her? I was invited round for tea and we all went out for a drink at the rugby club after. Despite winning the raffle that night I was not gonna get them to stay with me ever again. Hers was the place in vogue now. I was resigned to take the dregs, the left-over's the down and outs.

I was so happy when Yellow Rose, business woman of the year took on this lady for 4 nights. It started with her staying for one night and that she was waiting to be re-housed, by the council? This meant trouble, and it was to be. The sob story was out on the first breakfast morning. She had 'standby' *bi-polar*. It came when it suited her. Polar Bear was one minute normal then the next with no apparent reason a complete temperament change. I have seen this before and you have to get on top of these people or they will expose your weaknesses and play havoc with your life. This one was no exception. Poor Yellow Rose told me about this plighted woman. One who arrived carrying 2 black plastic bin liners containing her worldly comforts? She called her bag lady but my name is more appropriate, as the real bag lady comes later in the chronicles.

I had to help Rose out so I went to her aid. I sat and talked to Polar Bear for a while until I knew she was to go out. Rose took Polar Bear in her car to see if the social lady at the Christian help centre had any news for her, about her new accommodation. She hadn't so, still having to wait, Polar Bear gave Yellow Rose 3 more nights money. She looked like she had some money and wasn't flat broke. Yellow Rose has adopted our policy of no pay, no stay. It works.

This came at a price because Bear thought that if she paid up front then Rose was somehow obligated? She had already had a sympathetic ear from both of us and a free car ride to do her enquiry work. This was to escalate as now she asked if Rose knew of any flats for rent. I understand that the council will fund accommodation for waifs if they find something they like, within reason. Well Yellow Rose was up in this department as she herself for many years was in the same situation, renting studio flats on the wrong side of town. This was help she wanted to give Polar Bear. Then, out in Rose's car again they trolled over the other side of town and looked for estate agents to get a list of suitable flat-lets. All day doing this with no doubt refreshments along the way, Bear and Rose were on a mission.

Nothing was suitable as the next morning Bear came through for breakfast and was quite silent. In fact she started an awkward silence which was typical of the injured party making the host aware that it was all 'her fault'? What 'my fault', Yellow Rose uttered, that we couldn't find a flat for you? I spent all day looking and you had nothing to do but be driven from place to place. Right? Bear said, 'yes, it was pointless. I only want a council one bedroom flat, not any crummy old bedsit'? DOH! What not suitable? The silence descended again, Rose was shocked and breakfast was over. Bear retired to her room. The next morning I arrived for morning juice—don't ask? I talked to Polar bear, asking how she was. She definitely looked cleaner and had a lot better disposition. I asked if she had any news of her new flat and no, not yet. The pleasantries over, and with new optimism I said, 'what was the plan for today'? The plan was to go back to the Christian centre to see what progress had been made. Nothing was moving but the lady said that she could have a shelter accommodation for the time being. Well I don't know what this meant so I can only assume that it is definitely not as good as Yellow Rose's place. They left to see if this was suitable, and yes, Rose took her in her car again? The next I know is Bear and Rose having another awkward silence. This time I think that Bear is accusing Rose of kicking her out on the street, forcing her to take the subsidised Christian care accommodation, something she doesn't want. Rose has had enough! Day 4 and this is it. The weather is bad outside and Polar Bear is packed to go.

Standing in the door with her 2 bin bags she looked a sorry sight. How could Rose send her out into this with a clear conscience? Well I would! But no, Yellow Rose, softy that she is, (not with me I add)? She has to take her, by car again, to the centre. They are about to say their final goodbyes but no, the last insult, Bear said, 'can you give me your fiancée's phone number just in case I need accommodation again'? 'NO I can't. His place would not be suitable for you anyway'. With an enforced smile and limp wave Rose drove off.

Yellow is now mellow again and this episode had been further indication of the skills you need to run a Bed and Breakfast.

Chapter 12

The Outback man

He came to stay for 3 weeks. over here from Australia. His brief was to take the money his relation had left him in his will. The amount was relatively small but not insignificant as the trip to UK proved. It was his wish to revisit all his birth area had to offer. After all, 3 weeks is a long time doing nothing? There was another motive as he had not been here since he was a boy and knew nothing of the great city of London.

He was a bit rough around the edges not unlike what one would expect from an outback man, shorter than I imagined, beard, *corks dangling from his hat*, not kidding!

The first Rose had said about him was how clean he left the bathroom, but no, this was not true. The bathroom had not been used to shower or wash at all. Not even from the long haul flight he had endured. Only that the rim of the WC was splashed with urine and some had dribbled down the bowl to a pool on the new anti-slip vinyl flooring. This was horror of horrors for Yellow, as this yellow pee, (oops' didn't mean to use that as a simile), on the floor was absolutely filthy, slob yuck! 'Can't stand that for 3 weeks', she thought. What if the other guests go in there? What about only letting that floor to him and the bathroom to himself? This would be acceptable but wait, thinking. I will only have income from one up there and it can accommodate 5. So, he would be curtailing my income dramatically. This can't happen but how do I tell him?

21 Days of running up to check if 'Dribble' has control of his parts. What if I give him a little sighting lens he could fit on the end of it, and if I painted a little target on the bottom of the WC? He could aim and fire. Yes? No, he is used to the outback and aiming there is just downwind, anywhere. Dribble wouldn't do it. Dribble has a shaky hand.

She waited in fear to see if this problem disappeared, but it didn't. She had to check 4 times a day at least. The towels neatly prepared for guests still were not ruffled and the shower was pristine. Did Dribble ever wash? Absolutely filthy, slob, yuck!

Yellow thought he must wash sometime, what about his bed? Would I have to burn it? He didn't choose to have breakfast, and he came and went quietly so other than the yellow pool she didn't know he was there.

Well Yellow did detect a stale smoky smell coming from his room on her many visits up to his bathroom. Dribble smoked as well? Absolutely filthy, slob, yuck!

She was not going to go in there as she could imagine the abuse her nose would be subjected to.

A week passed and eventually there was the evidence, a screwed up towel on the floor with major grubby marks all over it. The shower base was a mess of grime with some thick black slimy substance trying to escape down the shower tray outlet. It was just hanging on to the chrome grid that stops hair from clogging it. What was this? She began to think perhaps it would be better to have him stay the way he is, unwashed, as this 'new' cleaning chore was worse than the yellow puddle. Rose was sick and urging.

She just had to grin and bear it. Other than this Dribble was keeping himself to himself until one day. He wanted some breakfast? Was this her time to talk a bit about things? During breakfast the conversation got onto his girlfriend in Oz. A photo was produced with pride. She was beautiful and had a dark gipsy look about her. Flamenco like, lustrous dark hair and slim body, a beauty. She thought, what was this 'babe' doing with this . . . 50 something year-old dirt encrusted man? Dribble had delusions of grandeur, surely? He was off to London today to Harrods. Rose was from London, working in the city for 16 years. This was not an easy place for Dribble to find by car. It's not like the outback.

Rose gave him instructions on the best route to take, where to leave the car, get the underground etc. He obeyed her knowledge and was successful as he returned with all the necessary bags full of London Tat. Just one thing stood out. He opened this dark green presentation box and inside was a diamond engagement ring? Rose was stunned as he announced with confidence his intention to marry Flamenco?

He leaves on Tuesday morning with his flight leaving London that evening

It would be another day or so when Rose will have visions of the two coming together in a loving embrace as he offers her the ring, from Harrods, how romantic. How utterly awful! How utterly unbelievable! How absolutely filthy, slob, yuck!

Chapter 13

Back to normal!

With Yellow Rose now secured and running her own B&B, we almost had the monopoly in the road apart from the one house I refurbished for some clients of mine back when I ran my building business.

I had a sign with my business name printed on and later adopted this to name my planned B&B. My web site was revamped to indicate my trade was no longer doing building services, and only offering accommodation, initially for students in family environments.

During my divorce the sign was removed coinciding with ill-health that stopped me from doing full-on building work and in fact anything for a while. As the clients wanted to run this new house as a B&B I gave them the sign and erected it for them to advertise their new business, but to my surprise they kept my trading name on the sign, and started trading in my business name, presumably thinking it would be appropriate to keep a familiar sign everyone locally new was there for years. Well I thought this was a cheek and a confrontation ensued in their garden. He squared up to me gritting his teeth not unlike the fish on the eucalyptus tree. With his fist in my face I saw the funny side and said to him, "don't be silly mate". This puny neighbour who had suffered a stroke in the past was told by his wife to put his fists down and to be reasonable as she knew he was no match for me, in fisticuffs. He retreated and the sign was renamed in something of their choosing. This left me purchasing a new sign, an illuminated one, and erecting it up where my original one was. Two signs up now and this was a red rag to the puny bull as this new better brighter and higher sign was in direct site line of his, and in no time the council arrived wanting the sign removed. How did they know? Well, not removed, just the illuminated part turned off, cos it was close to traffic lights and they said this would detract from them and possibly cause an accident.

I didn't contest this or seek planning permission to keep it, as I was just making my point, or was he just making his?

I have digressed as this lot happened before starting B&B 1.

Yellow Rose came back and forth between 1 and 2 for the next few months as she got to grips with her new life down here. It was strange cos just like me, she had to get used to complete strangers living in her house and it is worrying at first. Well it is always worrying but something you have to tolerate.

Then it started the feelings of being alone and scared. What if a male guest might have ideas about a woman being on her own? The locks had to be changed and added security was not easy. She wanted her own bathroom ensuite and her, 'personal space', apart from the rest of the letting rooms.

All my spare time was used up then revamping the old lounge in to a bedroom ensuite. A large shower base was fitted within the new studwork framing the new wardrobe. And a dropped ceiling with extractor fan fitted with down lighting and pull switch. The toilet had a masticator built under the floor to run the waste up and over to the main drainage on the other side of the house. Papering had to be redone and a new door had to be fitted in place of a window to get to . . . . yup! the new £8000.00 conservatory. This adjoined the kitchen extension to make the private area complete.

It is magnificent now and with all the effort, the marble floor, the electric thermostatically activated roof vent, the air con unit, plastering and painting the walls, the extra double radiator . . . it goes on.

She did get her way but she pulled her weight and was an able assistant, a good girl and worth it.

Now Yellow Rose is in the pink, money coming in and security when I am not there.

Back to normal then!

Chapter 14

The top floor, clean-up

Well, up the spiral staircase takes us to the vacated rooms last occupied by a Spaniard and his Romanian girlfriend. These 2 managed to leave the place uninhabitable for letting so I called on my mate's cousin, a youth of 16, to help with the clean-up. Stripping out the 'grey' carpet spotted with red dye left me with a great sense of utter waste. Maybe I was to blame a little for putting down a £ 24.50 per sq metre, thick pile sand coloured carpet in the first place. This surely was not suitable for a B&B but at the time it was our family home.

I left cousin youth to fill up the holes, remove the blue tack, strip out the ruined carpet and generally clear up the place prior to repainting.

That evening when the Spaniard returned to collect his left over items that wouldn't fit in his car, he was in very bad humour. His eyes flashed an enquiring dark Latin look and he said angrily, 'You lost me my new apartment by giving me a bad reference'? Well I said in reply, "No, I didn't. All I did was to tick boxes as they asked".

The only one which was detrimental to you was the one asking 'were the rooms left in good condition? I put an 'X'. All the other questions were answered positively with regard to honesty, paying on time, noise, etc. In fact the report was better than you deserve seeing the state you left this place in. My estimate for the clean up is around £1000.00. Would you like to pay for it? No? You weren't asked for a holding deposit when you first came to stay in my new top floor apartment? It is supposed to be left in the same condition as you found it? Nowhere near is it?

He left disgruntled, mumbling that I was not welcome at his forthcoming wedding to the Romanian. Well better I didn't go 'cos it would cost me a wedding present on top of the £1000.00 he didn't pay.

It's funny when someone who lives with you for some time like the Spaniard did, and all is going well between you, then when a third person comes into the equation, *the Romanian girlfriend,* it all went pear shaped. There it is? He loves her and I don't.

Repainted, spruced up with new fitted blue carpet, it was a week later the flat, as I call it now was ready for self catering occupation. It went immediately to a family of 3, mother, father and 9 year old daughter.

I know I said that this was gonna be bed and breakfast rooms but this family looked nice and they were just waiting for their new house to be made ready.

On the whole I didn't know they were there, quite quiet. Nipping up one day I made an effort to teach the little girl some magic to trick her friends, and to corrupt her a little. The parents had her 'under control' though. I asked her to lay her hand flat down on the table, palm up with fingers out straight and closed together. Then try to lift only her little finger vertical from the table, without moving any other fingers. It's hard,' Try it yourself, now', but to my amazement she did it. I tried another trick. We were sat around the dining table drinking black-current juice. I said to the family to do exactly what I do and if you can't you have to forfeit something. Easy peasy. This *trick* is usually performed in a pub to get free drinks. This is how. Take a sip of juice (or beer) swallow it and put down the glass. Lift the glass again and take another sip, swallow and move the glass to your other hand before you put it down. Following my lead so far? Finally pick up the glass again and take a sip. This time don't swallow, hold some juice in your mouth, put the glass down and push it away a little. (. Just little subtle changes for them all to copy) Pick it up again and spit the juice held in your mouth into the glass. Bingo!

I know disgusting? All the others would have swallowed their juice so you win. They can't copy you. Free drinks, well so much for my corruption!

They left after 6 weeks, their new home ready. They were a nice family, chatty and always bringing a progress report on how their new place was coming on. I often think about them especially when I see the triangle shaped iron mark burned into my new carpet.

It's worn in a bit now so they are becoming a distant memory.

Now the flat is free for the next lot, this time my plan is to have it as an overspill B&B on a self catering basis and with multi occupancy on short term arrangements. Workers for Monday through to Friday morning giving me time, or should I say the cleaning lady time, to strip all the beds and prepare for the young revellers at the weekends. This plan seems to be the most efficient way of using the space. So a large firm of tiling contractors took the flat for a year, a big tiling project in town, and the weekends were indeed free for the others. This was a great arrangement. It looked like all was starting to run smoothly and I could reduce the time I spent on the Bed and Breakfast side. The problem was the "one nighters". I was room cleaning and bed changing every day and the 'one nighters' wanted the Full Monty breakfast before 7.30 am to get away at 8. Well I am approaching 58 now and this routine was getting tiresome, so I sat down to actually work out what my profit the 'one nighters' brought. Well breakfasts cost £1.88 each for the ingredients, one fragmented hour to clean and change the room, wash dry and iron the bedding and put everything away. I estimated that as a builder I had earned £20 per hour. Using this formula it cost £21.88 plus wear and tear on the house, with gas, electric.water, rates etc. I figured I was about breaking even on the single occupancy. I was working for wages again?

Chapter 15

Day tripper

He was booked in and wanted a single room for one night. A one nighter was £30 including breakfast. The booking was taken over the phone and the enquirer asked where exactly is the B&B situated as the website wasn't clear. Yellow told 'Trippy', as he will be called, about the area and he confirmed it was just great. It was within walking distance of his venue, just across the road actually. The B&B was so perfect. He would pay cash on arrival.

Yellow Rose expected him to arrive at 6 pm this evening. Trippy did arrive on time and on entering dropped a bag from his grasp down onto her hall carpet with a derisory thump. This was not what Yellow expected as it made her jump. It was what put her on edge immediately. He then asked to see the room. Yellow wanted to book him in, but he wanted to see the room first.

Well this was irregular as he had booked, seen the web site and all she had to offer. He insisted so she offered him the downstairs single. All new, and adjacent to the shower room/wc. This was not suitable so she offered him another single room, this time he had the option of making his own tea and coffee as there was outside his bedroom, in a purpose built alcove, a sink unit complete with fridge, toaster, kettle, cups, plates, cutlery etc. not bad at all for a one nighter. On top of this was the adjacent bathroom which he was assured that was for his own use as no bookings were expected for the 'quad' room opposite. This was still not acceptable as he asked for a single en-suite room. Well by now Rose was annoyed as Trippy had rubbished her rooms as inadequate. He said, "Well, I suppose I will have to suffer the single upstairs". Red rag to the Rotty? Rose said in no uncertain terms that she was not going to book him in, and in fact he can go and find another B&B. She said, "you are a rude and objectionable little man and are not welcome to stay in my house."

This was a complete shock for Trippy as he had never been turned away before and he always got what he demanded. She would not consider his plea and told him again to get out, leave. He still resisted and said, "Where can I go at this time of night?" Rose replied, "You should have thought of that before you whinged out your orders. I don't care if you sleep in your car? The cost of the nearest hotel is £65. I know they have en-suites so go there. Cheerio."

Well, Yellow thought, what a misery, what a cheek, good riddance.

This was not the end of Trippy as I will reveal. His name was derived for 2 reasons. The first was the accident he had on the top step to the single room, without en-suite but with the sink option. He tripped slightly and nearly banged his head on the sink. Yellow giggled to herself. He should have done! Knocked some sense into him! Anyway, Trippy was not finished with Rose.

He wrote to Trip adviser. This is an internet site run on the Google Earth device for obtaining routes, places, and generally all things in the world. This asks travellers to write about their experiences when they stay at an establishment to allow other potential guests to evaluate the place. Could you imagine Trippy advising anyone to stay with Yellow Rose? I don't think so. You would be right.

Trippy wrote, "This is the worst place I have every stayed". Stayed??? "The landlady was the most aggressive I have ever met". Would I recommend this place for a romantic getaway? "No!" Would I recommend the position of the B&B? "No! The main road is noisy", He went to town and to justify his opinion by confirming he was the 'B&B Guru of Great Britain'. He said he has stayed at B&B's all over the UK so his views must be correct? The Trippy drippy dope didn't even stay the night, so how can he comment? Some people have delusions of grandeur?

His review is still on the web site so he had his gripe and that must make him satisfied, I suppose? Everybody who stays at Rose's place can't understand this idiot's review. Yellow Rose was satisfied, as that night he had to find alternative accommodation. Perhaps he did sleep in his car, awake all night planning his hate campaign?

PS. He didn't call me for B&B that night? Perhaps he had read my website first and knew I didn't have en-suites! He should have looked harder at Rose's website as she doesn't have them either. The Plonker!

Chapter 16

Bag lady

Not unlike Polar Bear she arrived at my B&B, in the pouring rain, with her bags, nylons rucked up, cardigan buttoned in the wrong holes. Water was dripping from her nose and the tall, skinny waif gave the necessary look to complete the sad picture. This was not fair as I didn't have the heart to turn her away. My B&B was so full up I took her to Yellow Rose's.

I was thinking again that this was to be nightmare on B&B Street 2. The sequel? She was not home so I let myself in and told bag lady to go and get a hot shower and get out of her wet clothes. I was hoping that Yellow still has the caring nature that I love, but will B&B life break into that good nature? We have already seen the Rottweiler comes out! So 'Baggy' she is then, and this is her story.

Baggy was cleaned up by the time Yellow arrived home from Yoga. She wondered what this wet-haired woman was doing drinking tea in her kitchen /diner. I explained that I was full and I didn't have room so would she take her in for a while. Having had an earlier experience with a dysfunctional person she was sceptical. True to form good old Yellow's nature came to the rescue.

I stayed and chatted for a while and left them together. Yellow told me that Baggy was married to an Australian? (Oh no? not corky hat), but it didn't work out so she left and relocated to Canada. She worked as a Nanny for some time in Canada and this is where she now called home.

Baggie's mother lives in England down in the West Country somewhere, along with her sister and brother. None of the family gets on with Baggy so she is alone. She had left her passport and other items of clothing with her mother with the idea to work here and there, make some money, revisit her family to recover her stuff and return to Canada. The reason she was in our care is that she took a job, in an affluent part of town, as a Nanny. The children's mother was of Eastern origin and the father was English. The family gave her a room in the house to be on hand to care for their 3 children. This job was just what she needed. A roof over her head, proper meals? Integrating with the family? She lasted just 4 days when they kicked her out, in the rain? Something was definitely not right here.

What did this woman get up to, to lose the job? Surely she can see that looking after people's children must have a 'trial' period and that she has to be on her best behaviour to give it a chance of success, or was it the family that didn't give her a chance. We will never know because Baggy lasted just 4 days with Yellow Rose. A pattern seems to be emerging here then? 'No pay no stay' is the motto so she had paid for 4 nights and had run out of money. As a last ditch resort Rose told Baggy to 'pack up', but leave her bags in the hall.

She would go over the road to the 'House of Destiny' . . . a charitable church that try and help homeless people and the like. Well this was difficult as she was skint now and the time to get her a place in one day was not feasible. Here Rose is again, being Piggy in the middle with these people's problems. They get themselves in these fixes every time and rely on the good natures of others to bail them out.

Baggy, came back and said, "No good at the Destiny place". So she left, we know not where?

Yellow Rose has now said that she will "never ever, ever take anybody in who has not got a suitcase, proper clothes, car and a very good reason for staying."

Wow, a lot of conditions? I will wait and see.

Chapter 17

The holiday we both deserve

With both B&B's 1 & 2 running smoothly it was time to go on that big holiday together. As usual I was not completely closing down for the 2 weeks but Yellow Rose was. On the Friday morning a young lad from the north arrived on the doorstep requesting a room for 3 nights. Well as we were off on a Caribbean cruise at lunch time this day I didn't see I could take him. The lad was cleanly dressed, new trainers jacket etc and had a pleasant face. He didn't want breakfast as he was visiting his dad who he used to live with locally, but didn't get along with his dad's 'new' lady partner. I thought as he didn't want breakfast and I had a permanent lodger who stood 6 foot 4 inches tall and built like a barn door I was fairly sure no any harm would come to my place. He paid £105 cash, £35 per night. We left for the boat.

We left port at 6.30 in the evening with the usual ticker tape and band offering? All the relatives of the passengers were cheering and waving at the quayside making sure this was a grand send off.

We settled down to an evening of lovely food and calm anticipation of the trip. First checking out our cabin and then testing each facility to see what was on offer. We were like kids with new toys . . .

The first port of call was Madeira where the weather changed to a balmy 22 degrees, blissfully unaware of the happenings at home. We could be contacted but it is difficult at the best of times and anyhow I didn't want to be bothered.

I could go on about the Caribbean islands for a whole book but suffice to say it was great. We got a flight back from Barbados directly to London and travelled down by bus from there. On arriving home the place was quiet, nothing was burned down and all seemed to be in order. Then the Bigfoot came thumping down the stairs and told me all. Apparently this is what happened.

My son had a little lifelike pea-shooting gun which fired plastic peas. The thing looked real enough and you could have an eye out if you shot someone with it. He was warned but, as lads are, he shot his mate in the bum just to hear him squeal and it was duly confiscated.

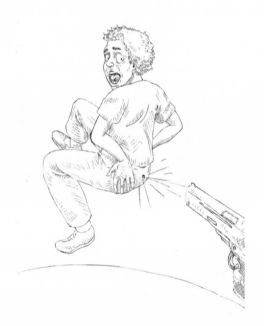

It was in a plastic bag on the floor of the kitchen at the bottom of the stairs to room number 4. This room was occupied by our smart youth. The police were called and arrived at the house with silent approach at 5 am on the Sunday morning. *We were just about in the middle of the Bay of Biscay by then.* There were 7 police cars, the Police chief constable, support officers and a 4 man swat team wearing boots and flack jackets. A woman police officer woke Bigfoot and asked which room the youth was in. "Number 4" he said and 3 burly police officers slowly climbed up the stairs to the room as quietly as they could. Bigfoot was in his underpants being quizzed by the police lady under the car port.(not to be recommended). Within 5 minutes the cops came down with the youth securely handcuffed and led him away. Bigfoot was allowed back to his room.

The lad was a bit silly as he had been out drinking that night and without consent, brought an under aged girl home with him.

I had something sexual happen before this when staying in the single room, now occupied by Bigfoot. A young lady, 22 or so, brought back an unsanctioned bloke to her room. They must have crept in after midnight when I was fast asleep. The man probably was paying for her services, as she came from somewhere up country. I only took £30 for her 1 night stay. That morning she came for breakfast alone and I suspected nothing. At breakfast she said she might want to stay another night. She phoned me later in the day and said she would stay for a second night and pay me at breakfast time as she would be in late again. I went to bed that evening and didn't awake until I heard my outside door open, with the buzzer alarm sound and looking out my bedroom window I saw both of them creeping away from the house. It was 6 am in the morning.

She was escaping without paying. She had her guest with her and both were leaving without paying. One of them, I suspect him, who carefully removed the little chimes above the door to alert me when this particular door is opened. Her guest was paying her, not me, the cheek! Prostitution occurring in my home, something that I was not going to permit!

The young lad police took away had raped this under aged girl, at gun point, and after he fell asleep she crept downstairs, left the house and alerted the police, who arranged the dawn raid. This was a serious matter, a rape, a gun, how did he possibly think he was going get away with it?

At school when he found out about the raid, my son 'the digger driver' told all his friends. His rendition was a little more colourful. It went . . . The police smashed down the door shouting, "Get down! Stay down!" they were spraying the place with bullets, kicking in the door, capturing the suspect and beating him to the ground then dragging him down the stairs with him screaming his innocence.

Should have blamed myself for this as it was I who left the gun and peas on the floor and without that, the youth's scheme of terror would not have happened. I had to laugh as 3 weeks later the rapist's dad came round to collect the money for the 1 night his son was in police custody. What about that for a family? I gave it to him as he looked a bit rough and obviously had no qualms of asking for the son's money back. Most people would have been too ashamed to even come to the door let along ask for a refund. I didn't want repercussions over £35.

Chapter 18

Bigfoot!

He arrived almost as soon as the single room was readjusted from the earlier incident. The room was fresh and although small, just enough to get a bed in. The eaves beams are close to your head when leaning over the bed. Well Bigfoot wanted a room for a while during his engineering contract for a local machine shop.

He took the room. I was surprised as he was a giant of a man with ruddy, young-looking face and deep booming voice as if he was shouting. He settled in and at first he was quite good to talk to telling of his travels, his relationship with a Spaniard—Oh no, they get everywhere. This one was a lady he lived with for 12 years in South Africa—not again! He said he loved her and they ran a steak house together for some years. He loved her cooking and he wanted me to affirm this as he offered to cook me her recipe for tortilla. This was filling and I agreed that it hit the spot. 12 eggs and a whole packet of potatoes, cooked in 2 full sized fry pans and one portion each, Gut bustin spot!

It all seemed amicable until it happened. Another trip to the hospital. His breathing was shallow and his legs were a mess of blotches. His feet were black but I suspected this was from the black oily residue he stood in all day whilst machining up his bits. It probably was as a trail of footprints went from the bottom of the newly carpeted staircase across the small landing to his room. This is not why he is called Bigfoot.

I had to drop the roof down on the sports car as he was too tall and his head was at least 1 foot above the windscreen.

I asked if he would like to wear my ski hat with the bobble on. He declined. So on the way down to A&E, I watched as his 3 or 4 strands of long black hair flitting around in the wind. Concerned that I was gonna loose another guest this time I waited at the hospital. All was ok except that loads of tests were to be performed and he had to return the next day with a bag of toiletries and clothes to change into.

After a week of tests Bigfoot said he had left without a change of underpants and wanted me to bring some in for him. I obliged as instructed to rummage through his little room to find a stack of large raggedy frayed blue/grey underpants in a heap under his bed. I grabbed a handful and got straight down to the hospital. His heart monitor registered 133 beats per minute however when I arrived and he got up from his bed it went up to 165. Wow I thought can I really do this to another human and would I have the same effect on Yellow Rose?

During this time I removed the new stair carpet that left the stair treads with an unusually dark stain finish. The stairs are Brazilian pine—a reddish wood—previously stained Jacobean oak nearly black. They have open treads and small retaining rails at the back so children can't get their head stuck between them . . . The paint and grain I chose was English pine so it had a calm creamy beige look. I also tackled the oily footprints on the landing to his room by cleaning off the new dark yellow carpet with a scrubber filled with fairy liquid, bleach and water. I was expecting on his return that with feet now washed and cleaned the new arrangement would last for some weeks before the oil trails appeared again. I suggested that he wore slippers from now on as the treads were no longer carpeted.

Yes, Bigfoot arrived back home carrying 2 bags. One was full of underpants and the other was full of tablets and pills and a list of foods he could no longer have. Among this list alas was not his favourite food, the disgusting tinned squid in tinta, that's the squirty black inky stuff squids spit out at an aggressor. Another was some nameless strong Italian cheese he's partial to, that smells like some filthy old boots worn by a tramp for a year. His diet was surprisingly not to include cranberries, pine-apple, and other things; however he didn't offer to give me his supply of banned tinned fruit stacked under his bed.

In celebration of his return a week later Bigfoot went out on his favourite Friday night, trip to the local pubs. He arrived home on the last bus at 11.15pm. He went upstairs and got undressed. He came back down to get a hot drink before retiring. He always has this routine as I can see the kitchen light come on. I had just got into my bed and was startled by an almighty crack followed by the sound of falling timber rattling on the kitchen tiles. Comfy in my bed although roused I thought no, I will investigate that in the morning. The first rays of sun streamed through my Venetian slats and I awake immediately remembering last night's crack. Getting up quickly, the first thing I do is to look at what happened. Well the evidence was on the floor, a broken back rail of the 5th stair up and the crash was this falling onto the ceramic tiles. He had come home a bit happy and carefree but not in control of his size 14 feet, and because the treads are now bare of carpet he lost his footing and thrust his big toe straight through the back of the stairs Being somewhat deaf and worried about spilling his hot drink he didn't even know he did it. Poor chap.

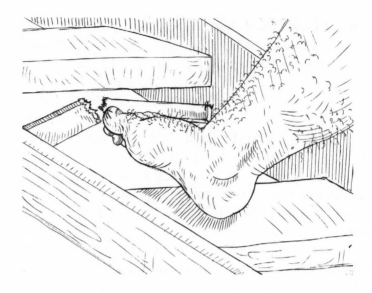

Dressing properly I got to picking up the 2 halves of the rail and to my surprise they fitted together on the break and they slotted back in to place perfectly. All I had to do was glue the fracture and re paint and grain it. Done. Hence the name Bigfoot! To this day I have not spoken of this incident but I suspect he has selective memory loss on the subject and wouldn't admit he broke the stairs anyway! It was funny though because that morning at breakfast I accidently brushed across his toe sprawled under the table to which he let out a big yelp! Bit tender was it?

Chapter 19

The other Hotel guest

This guest came from another part of town early on in my B&B start up. Some friends who own and run a mid sized hotel had a taxi driver who stayed with them. He wanted to come over this side of town to be more central to his base. My hotel friend also told me that he was slow at paying and £20 was hard for him to afford. Well I took him on a trial basis by offering him a bed in the chalet. This is a wood structure at the bottom of my garden with a veranda. The view is looking up the garden towards the house. This is not a bad view and the reason I took him on was that this was a new venture for me and I was eager to maximise my income. This suited him as he worked nights and he was always being disturbed with the movements and door banging of the cleaners. Here, he had to do that himself, self-catering. The cost was the same as the hotel so all I had to do was keep an eye on him paying the rent on time.

I called him 'shed man'.

It was handy having your own taxi driver on hand so the guests would not have to wait around and he knew how to get home at night. All was good and payments started to flow frequently.

As time went by shed man found a Brazilian girlfriend who was eager to date him, He obliged and within 2 days of seeing her she wanted to move in with him. He said where he lived was not suitable for 2 but she had to see for herself. They arrived and this small and bubbly dark haired girl of about 35 appeared with shed man He had a big beaming smile over his face, showing his pleasure with this highly attentive female draping herself over him. She said she had 2 sons in Brazil, she worked as a carer and lived in, but these old people seemed to die on a regular basis so soon she would need another job, perhaps without being able to live in. A need for suitable living accommodation for both would soon dawn it they were to live together? Did I mention the 2 son's?

She said she would like to do cleaning as an auxiliary job, and as I had a vacancy for this I thought I could help. Yellow Rose had her own cleaning to do and I was not up to do my work. I preferred a cleaner like Yellow or my original one, (My ex wife's best friend), who had other things to do now her elderly aunty needed a helper.

I agreed a rate for her pay and she was to start the next week. Yellow Rose was not pleased and said, "Cleaning Lady would not be up to scratch, nobody, cleans like me"? Well time would tell but I knew that she would be right, she always is.

A few weeks passed and shed man did leave the chalet and together they moved into an ex-council flat, rented out by the owner for £650 per month. plus bills. They had no furniture so I gave them my old baggy suites which had similar cushions but with differing colours, one pink, one grey, and the other cream. I thought if these cushions and arm rests were rotated to mix them a harlequin effect would make them less conspicuous if viewed in the same room. It did in a way as all the carpets and existing wallpapering in the flat were a miss-mash of colours anyhow. So happy families, but there was a dark cloud coming.

Shed man said he was happy and they had talked about getting married. I didn't like the idea as I knew she only wanted to get a passport to remain in the country. She went back to Brazil to visit her 2 son's and stayed with them for a while. Sorting out things I suppose. Cleaning for myself again . . . would Yellow help me?

Next I know Cleaning Lady is back in the UK again and this time wedding plans are being discussed. We are the first to be told and a date was imminent. It was so quick that I didn't think there was any time to organize a reception.

It was a quiet affair though in the local registry office and pictures were taken on various mobile phones and afterwards a little 'doo' in the evening at a local restaurant. All was rosy and this was exactly what she wanted. A British husband and now the long wait to get the 2 year acceptance from the home office. Would it last, no chance??? She is back cleaning for me, same rate as before although she wanted more! Cost of the living accommodation they have, no doubt?

A new shed man arrived, "my name is Rogers", he said, "Lord Buck Rogers actually". Yes, right . . . Buck Rogers, bleepy, bleepy, bleep.

The Lord was the new resident in the shed, sorry chalet, newly named, 'Buck-enham Palace'. Garden annex!

It was strange I had a 'real' Lord staying in my shed! I told everyone, nobody believed me. I was sceptical but he showed me indentures, duly notated and signed on parchment type paper with the Royal crown embossed in gold. He also had e-mails of newspaper clips for his achievements. He had a credit card in his name. Everything on the surface gave me no reason to suspect anything was wrong. Just think, my B&B by royal appointment. I thought of payments. Get the money in cash, 'no pay no stay', that's my motto.

One morning Lord Buck must have spied Cleaning Lady working in the flat so on that morning he took to sitting in my kitchen drinking coffee after coffee. Cleaning lady wisped in the side door to the kitchen. She opened the sink cupboard and rummaged around to find some cleaning fluid. She bent over to look in the cupboard, directly in full view of us, her tight pants revealing a white thong strap and a tattoo low on her back.

Buck liked this as I saw his face light up, although he tried to conceal it. She stopped to talk to us and after some banter she carried on with the cleaning and he left to go back to his shed. She finished work for the day and I gave her cash, a £20 note, for 3 hours 20 minutes of work @ £6.00 per hour. 20 of those minutes she was talking with Buck and me. That talking cost me 2 quid?

I didn't give this another thought as time went by, but original shed man did cos it was only 3 weeks later when he came in and said, "I'm not happy". "What's the problem?" I said. He explained that Cleaning Lady was not being truthful to him and wouldn't tell him what she was doing with the money he was giving her. He questioned her about it. I said, "Maybe it's because she is missing her sons back in Brazil and she would like them to be with her. Perhaps she is sending the boys more money than you know? She did say to me that she misses her boys." Well, he had to go as the taxi device he carried around sounded off and he was required to leave immediately.

The next week I did maintenance on number 2 B&B. I left the money in a jar for Cleaning Lady to take when she finished. At about 2.15 in that afternoon she arrived and sat outside number 1. She saw me and shouted from her car window, "Wot's this then"? I went over and saw she was holding £18 worth of one pound coins. "I am not accepting this rubbish". "What's wrong?" I said. "I only want notes, not shrapnel!" she grumbled. I replied that I didn't have an £18 note to give her the correct money. '3 hours @ £6 per hour is £18', I said? "I left you the full amount in coins!" She said, "You should have given me a £20 note and we would sort it out next week". "Oh no, you get paid what you earn." She said, "I won't be coming back next week then, I'm finished working here! I have another job I want anyway." and drove off in a huff!

I did the cleaning again and I didn't see shed man for a while either.

Eventually, shed man did call to see me, with *her, Cleaning Lady's,* mobile phone in his hand. He said, "Take a look at this"." It showed a picture of her inside Madam Tussauds, in Birmingham? He said". "I'm very confused, what's all this all about?" Well she had gone to Birmingham to see her Brazilian girlfriend on the Tuesday, just like that, without warning and would be back on the Saturday night. Shed man was to pick her up at the railway station near by at 12.15 am precisely? Ok shed man confirmed, on Saturday at 12.15 she was not there to be picked up. So as a suspicion shed man, now (Taxi man), called to where Lord Buck had moved in recently, his new penthouse flat. This flat was close to this railway station where he arranged to meet Cleaning Lady. He drove to see if Buck's car was there. It was, so waiting for a few minutes, who do you think turned up in another taxi? Lord Buck, himself and alone! Buck inquired, "what are you doing here at this time of night?" to Taxi man. Taxi made an excuse saying that he had just dropped of a fare and was waiting for another call. I know Buck knew different?

Going up the road Taxi man stopped the other cab and asked the driver where he picked Buck up, and he replied, the train station. Oh Yeah? *Not the one his wife agreed to meet, but another station about 6 miles away nearer his house.* Asking the taxi driver, "was there any one else in the taxi, with the man?" He said "yes, a woman who he dropped off first" and . . . would you know it, at Taxi mans own home address!

The deception was proved, Taxi man, seething now raced home. Opening the front door she said convincingly, "where were you at 12.15 then?" Complaining she had to get her own taxi home. He didn't let on, but questioned her further. She said she was in Birmingham with her girlfriend. She was not in Birmingham as the photo on the phone dated on the Wednesday, 3 days earlier in the week proves that she was in London. They have no Madam Tussauds in Birmingham. Caught in the act then and to cunningly say to pick her up at one station when knowingly be with Buck at another, ensuring that they would not be caught. It was all planned from the start. Cunning but not cunning enough for our taxi sleuth eh!? She confessed that she and Buck did stay together but insisted that they had separate rooms, Yeah, Right? And nothing ever happened, Yeah, Right?

This sad affair was not over. Taxi man has had this happen to him before. The first 'wife', he married, left him, taking all his savings and leaving him shattered and bankrupt. This is going the same way? It is strange he is attracted to these immigrants, the first one being Bulgarian. His problem might be the letter 'B',

Bulgarian, Brazilian. Perhaps he should stick to someone from England maybe from Birmingham! Nasty quip that.

He keeps in touch but has said he wants to be left alone to work out his mess. You know at one time he actually accused me of breaking up his marriage to Cleaning Lady by . . . introducing her to Lord Buck? Love twisted mind eh!

Chapter 20

The Buckaroo story

He wanted to stay with Yellow Rose. She recognised him as the strange man who asked her earlier if he could stay at her B&B. She sized him up said that at this time her 2 singles rooms were taken. She lied? She thought to herself that this slightly creepy individual was not the sort she wanted in her new establishment.

So he had been trawling the streets for suitable accommodation and I know he had walked past by my place as it was on the way to number 2. Yellow Rose confirmed he told her, hers would have been his first choice to stay, presumably because a lovely blonde might be a good score for him.

I will let you make up your own mind.

I took him in for an indefinite period but he did have an agenda as he said that he was waiting for his new apartment to be finished so he could bring his new fiancé back from her working position in Spain. He said they were to be married, in the autumn.

He moved in to the shed and as previously written I renamed it Buck-enham Palace. I like my little joke as it becomes a little bumpy sometimes running a simple B&B and this lightens my mood.

The Lord Buck washed himself in one of the upstairs shower rooms and took his gear back down the garden path before coming back in for breakfast. He was a healthy eater but he did smoke and despite his best efforts to conceal this, stale smoke did emanate slightly from his clothes.

He always dressed as you would expect a Lord would, perhaps with the exception of the eccentric colourful Lord Bath! He wore smart clothes of various styles, usually dark coloured with shoes of polished leather with clippie clop heels, solid sounding when he walked anywhere. His head was held high and he had an air of importance about him. He talked with an accent. One just couldn't put a finger on 'which' public school . . .

He said, he had letters after his name, well we all do don't we? Mine letters are I-D-i-O-t! Joking aside his were impressive. A PhD in accountancy and a few other jumbled alphabet characters I didn't take much notice of. This, he said, he used for his main income and that he worked for a familiar world wide accountancy firm, as a consultant. Sometimes he made it clear as he was speaking on his mobile within earshot, when he talked loudly about important high finance issues regarding his clients. He said they paid him handsomely for his efforts, especially about this one important call. He successfully negotiated with some bank executive a large amount in refunds for the banks mishandling of his client's money. He boasted that he received £6000.00, for this effort . . . . Yeah, right?

It was becoming clear that Lord Buck needed some research on my part as I wanted to know if he was a genuine lord! As you know he had on arrival showed all the necessary credit cards and proof of who he was and as this was an unusual situation the emails he sent me and the written evidence of his knighthood.

The first step was to check out his name from the police records. I do not have access to these records but I know a man who does. This turned up an answer of sorts. My man said he couldn't disclose any details but, "All I can say is don't take a cheque from this guy!"

So fraud looked possible, but as yet no criminal records were evident. Lord Buck was 2 points down now and so more delving was required.

The next was to check into who was in the lists of Lords, currently alive, and there were 3 Lord Rogers at the time. None of these are named Buck, and as their photos confirm none look like Buck either. Certainly none claimed to live in sheds. 3 points down now!

The next thing was this email he insisted on sending me. The first told of his excellent track record in raising a staggering 2.5 million pounds for the orphan's hospitals in Romania. This was raised by the charity challenge annually his company ran worldwide. He was the individual this year, nominated to collect for the charity he put forward. This took some time to achieve but with his contacts within the firm he encouraged them all to gather money on his behalf.

The newspaper clips were convincing, telling of the above and how the queen knighted him along with another famous person in some other field of equal achievement. It was done well but contacting the newspapers involved and looking at their headlines for the day and date, no such article was there. A fraud then! 4 points down now maybe 5. Two for that scam.

The other email clip was just reporting the amount raised and praising him for his efforts. Again no such article in the paper. Good old Buckee! 6 points down and the evidence building.

The fiancée he was to marry was the next problem. He showed me his, 'Facebook folder' and produced her photo amid 50 or so others he claimed as 'friends'?

A rather plump lady was on my screen. He said her name and that she worked in Spain, managing a string of time shares or something. Managing the cleaning of these time shares and getting them ready for the next guests arrival. It was an important job which held a good income.

I asked, "At her age was she really going to jack the job in to live with you. What would she do?" "She is trained in law as a legal secretary", he said, Right? Legal secretary working as a cleaner! Right! Perhaps she could work for me as cleaner 'Lady Rogers'?

Time went by and before moving into his brand new penthouse apartment, Buck invited me to view it. In my capacity as an ex builder he naturally wanted to ask my advice on certain things.

We went in his new, large second hand BMW saloon, suitable for a Lord as his old Astra was on its last legs. His old car had been sold to my ex-cleaning lady for £400. She was to pay him when she could. Right!

The place was brand new a year before and he was waiting for the residents to end their term. This had left the light cream shag pile carpet slightly soiled and dented around the space where the dining table legs were. The apartment was void of all furniture except for a TV and a couple of cream leather settees. It did look good though, a large open plan kitchen/diner/lounge off the central hallway, with a door leading to an inner hall with the 2 bedrooms and communal bathroom between. The place was handily situated within walking distance into town. I would have bought the place if I was in the market for a penthouse in town flat.

We talked as we walked about the place, it was in the roof of the block, and the day was hot. The temperature was unusually over 90 degrees. I opened the roof windows and said this would be a problem both in summer and winter as the insulation was inferior and the winter cold would be a problem especially for plump Spain. I didn't see any gas hob or radiators so the flat was all electric then! No central heating?

I offered a discounted new Air con unit, one that would provide hot as well as cold air. The thing runs on little power and was good for the environment, no emissions. He thought about it and ordered a stand alone unit that required no fixings to the fabric of the building. After looking and getting a feel for the place we come back home. I still have this unit, un-wrapped in my garage to this day!

Later Taxi Man comes on the scene and tells me that Buck has offered her, his wife, Cleaning Lady a position doing his cleaning and other tasks to do with accountancy, addition, filing etc, on the computer. I wonder what Lady Buck will make of that?

The work would pay well and she would be required to do it around her other duties as a carer, evenings mostly? Right! Cleaning lady would be able to go to Bucks 'new penthouse palace' easily as she has his old car and still owes him the money for it no doubt, Cosy eh? I didn't hear from our Buck after the move but we did meet much later at a garden party. Taxi man and cleaning lady were having a get together. We knew he was attending, so I and Yellow Rose wanted to go for the fun. You see this garden party brought all the protagonists together and we wanted to be involved with the occurrences. And they did occur.

First before we arrived I understand that one of Taxi man's best friends wife had cleaning lady's head jammed in the open oven, over a disagreement that nearly ruined the whole event. Singed hair does that! All the woman attending were asked to prepare some food for this barbeque and the resulting reheating/cooking between them got fraught in cleaning lady's tiny kitchen.

On arrival we looked around all the guests but didn't see Lady Buck anywhere.

Bucko was sat centre table directly opposite cleaning lady and Taxi man. She, as usual in company, was perched on her hubby's lap apparently with no cares in the world. Bucko must have been seething over this show of 'false affection', but he hid it well only shifting his nonchalant leg from one knee to the other occasionally talking to the others to his right and left.

We positioned ourselves away from the main table now full of friends and sat to the right hand side of Buck and slightly to his rear. This didn't move him but he looked uneasy as he started shifting more when I asked "Where is Lady Buck?" We were on his case and he knew his ruse was up. We left early, leaving the stragglers to their misery. The atmosphere was dreadful despite cleaning lady's bubbly goings-on. I would no doubt get the lows of the day from Taxi Man.

I think you know the result of all this as in the earlier episode the facts came out and although devious dealings were going on nothing concrete could be proven at this time. We stayed in contact with Taxi Man mostly but we were both getting a bit disillusioned with the continuing façade he offered us. Taxi Man was in a dreadful position and he could not find an answer to his dilemma. He had firm feelings of love for cleaning lady and she could, at will, wrap him around her little finger. This will break Taxi man as he desperately wants *this* marriage to work. Poor old Taxi Man!

"Buck you are the lowest of humanity, proved to be a charlatan, a liar and fraudster. You have no regard for Taxi Man's plight." Mrs Buck Rogers is nowhere on the scene?

You tell me she called the wedding off. It was never on?

You even said you kept your smoking from her. You are joking aren't you?

That would never be the case unless she was deaf, dumb, and blind, with no other sensory organ except her tonsils.

The arrangements for your reception, the 5 star Hotel, the agreement that the local police would close the road during the bride and grooms arrival? The wedding dress code, chosen from the choice you brought me from the high class wedding rental shop? Inviting me to choose, for you, the colour to theme the thing and making sure we were invited as honoured guests near, or on, the top table? Along side this rubbish, telling of a second London affair, with grand garden marquee, erected in Hyde Park, Mayfair, to re-celebrate the wedding reception for all the high class guests you know, including certain ministers of this current parliament. I even think you mentioned some lower royals. What a load of bollocks!

Writing this has almost made me annoyed.

I think your total points, has topped 20. You're busted Mr Buck Rogers, Bleepy-bleepy, bleep.

Through all this I didn't lose any money and he didn't take anything from me. The sad thing is that the owner of the apartment reported that Bucko owed him £3000 for the rent. A bounced cheque I reckon?

You know, I think if Cleaning Lady and Bucko do get it together they DESERVE each other.

Chapter 21

Moving man!

He was a clean pleasant man with tight cut ginger hair. He has an easy personality that was eager to please. He would help with anything asked of him and it seemed that he had time on his hands. He was the new long term occupant of any room that was available as guests dictated. He would move from a twin room to the apartment if guests wanted certain requirements. Eventually he ended in the shed, like all the others. This was because he got slow with the payments. He went about his business and I didn't inquire what he did. One morning in the kitchen he said he was a part time amateur referee for the local clubs. Affiliated to the FA He got paid a small salary for this semi-professional role. This kept him fit, but poor.

He was always interested in the ladies and was very pleasant when Yellow Rose was about. In fact this is when he came alive. I have told you of his help in extracting Yellow Rose from her London house. This is the story he told me on the long trip up the 140 miles. In a nutshell, he said that his wife wanted divorce and was kicked out from his family home. The wife was bringing up their only child, a boy of about 12 I think. This left him homeless and he moved back to his Mother's house, drifting from girlfriend to girlfriend. He had to get something of his own as his elderly mother and father had their own life and didn't want their grown-up son, pleasant as he was, living with them. They lived close by and so my B&B was handy.

Out of misguided sympathy I allowed some, 'missed payments' as he was always asking to do things about the house for rent money. After a while this was not sustainable and he had to get some real form of work.

We arrived in London and started to disassemble Yellow Rose's possessions and placing them flat packed in the large trailer I had borrowed from a mate. This work was pretty intense so that evening I treated us all to a night at the local Indian. A group of girls on a hen night or some such outing sat behind us, in close proximity, in the cramped restaurant. We ordered Tiger beer and a variety of Indian food. The girls loved our carefree ways and soon jokes were being exchanged, risqué jokes and the interaction became as one group. Moving man was on the periphery but laughing with us all. His joy was apparent but he just left all the banter to the rest of us, just sitting in the corner. On leaving Yellow Rose pulled me by the groin out and away from the laughing hens. I had quipped about being single and as I followed her grip, in earnest, one hen for good measure pinched and patted my bum to send me on my way. All this amused moving man and he said that this was one of his best evenings out for a long time. He had a need for some solidarity in his life and our relationship, that is mine and Yellow Rose's was perfecto.

Arriving back at night to her stripped out house, it looked unloved. The personal items that make up a home were packed away. All the unnecessary clutter was gone, the soul of the house gone with it. Yellow Rose was leaving and it must have affected her as this is where she had lived and played for some years and now it was time to go. Some tears were expected after the hilarity of the evening. Moving man was dismissed to the spare room still sporting the put-u-up which was his comfort for the night. Mine was cuddling the hot bare flesh of Yellow Rose that soon lapsed into pleasant dreaming, our work for the day, done.

The morning brought the cold light of day, curtain less and stark. We got on with the bed removal, still warm from the night before and made final adjustment to the overloaded trailer. The last look from the road brought the inevitable tears and we were gone. The stop for toilets at the motorway services was soon upon us as we barely had 40 miles on the clock. Would we make it the rest of the way without stopping again?

Was this nerves or something women have that I knew nothing about, one hour toilet breaks?

Back to moving man then. He was still spritely on arriving home and this was only the start of the drama to unfold. The contents of the trailer, van and car were to be unloaded into and around my B&B. Her stuff took up the rest of the lounge and encroached into the dining room The garage was full of non-perishable items and my clothes resting in my, *now our*, main bedroom wardrobes were considerably thinned out and re-arranged.

Moving man was not as comfortable with this part of the operation as he was no doubt recalling his experience earlier by sorting out clothes from his ex-home. The job was done and after a cuppa he retreated to the shed. FA headquarters!

On our way up it also came to light that he was seeing a prostitute who he had feelings for. He would have moved in with her but as she was still active in the field, well in her bed actually, and so it would be impossible for that to work. Just think of the scenario? "Hello darling would you like a cuppa . . . Oopps sorry I didn't know you had . . . . company"? Well he could referee?

Everyone he met had some other agenda and he was appearing to me that he amounted to a being a gigolo. Was this the work that gave him his added small income or was it something else? He admitted that he would visit a high class bars looking for women. These women usually had a bob or two so the drinks were on them in exchange for his company. He thought what if I could get one of these lonely women to care for me, give me access to their homes, their car, their wealth, in exchange for my loyalty, my body? He was arm candy for women.

This was the situation one day when he turned up in a black shiny car. He said, he might have a new 'permanent residence', house sharing with our lonely bar lady with her diamond rings, suntan and designer clothes! With a beaming smile of those flashing white teeth he explained this was his new lady friend's car and how he had to transport her from place to place, acting as her chauffeur. He was expecting to live in. This was it, the big score. Only 3 days later, an unhappy fat woman drove up outside my place in the black shiny and deposited Moving man onto my driveway along with his suitcase. He was back to square one or should I say FA headquarters.

As time went by he had started to run up a rent bill and despite his assurances he would get the money, this last scam was a no go, so he had no pay. What happened to 'no pay, no stay'?

One day he asked if his son could stay and asked if I would not talk of the fat lady. I assured him I would keep quiet so the boy arrived.

He said he had a new job with a large betting organisation and would be based in Southampton. The job came with a car and it was being delivered here on Saturday afternoon. Seeing his son for the morning and getting a new car in the afternoon things were looking up. He had worked in this field before for another betting chain so his salary would pay off his debt to me quickly. Just think a car, a job, money coming in. Great!

Moving man wanted to move out of the shed into the flat so he could do more with his son and perhaps have him stay over. This was OK after the deficit of rent was paid off. He agreed. The son arrived for a morning visit as this Saturday was his last weekend before he started work. The car was arriving from the bookmaker's and then things would be good. He waited and I waited but the car didn't materialise so where is it, travelling to Southampton on the train was not an option. He phoned someone to find out where it was but they were not there. Another rent period came and went and so I added up the deficiency and it was over £ 1000. Well, shock, as I thought this is wrong.

On the Monday I decided to check up on a few things myself as I was suspecting untruths were being told. I phoned the

Southampton Office and asked if Moving man was there as he said he had been taken on last week and was travelling up on the train. Moving man who? They said. No new employees have been taken on and certainly no new managers. This was strange but not surprising as now he was proved to be a liar. I phoned his elderly mother and said that her son has been staying with me for some time and he was behind with the rent. Could she help as the debt was now £1000?

She said, "We have nothing to do with him anymore because he just keeps bringing this sort of problem back with him, so we had no choice but to kick him out for good. Please don't ring again!"

I waited until Moving man came back from his, 'new job'. He arrived with a sheepish look as if he knew something was going to happen. It did. I took him to the bottom of the garden to the patio and told him straight of the deception he spread. I told him of the phone calls to the bookies and to his mother. He looked genuinely shocked that I went to these lengths to expose him. He lives and breathes lies and lives in a Walter Mitty world, preying on the next unsuspecting victim. There is no law for this type of deceit. It is up to the individual to rescue all they can from the situation. In my case just the money and to this end he promised to repay all he owed.

He did keep his word for a while, turning up with teeth grinning, in a very clean, shiny new Vauxhall. He pressed £100 in my hand saying more next week as he was now working. Then, after a couple of weeks the payments stopped. He still owes over £750.

Where is Moving man now? Still trying to make it without working I suspect. He doesn't keep in touch, they never do. When there is a chance of a meeting I would never know, because these people see me first, are always alert to the danger of being collared, and disappear quickly. How can this existence be favourable? What drives them to lie and live like that?

Chapter 22

The Australians!

I will keep this short as this episode did make me mad. It was mid-summer and the internet brought forth our distant criminal relations, the Aussies. They spoke of renting a family room, for 3 nights, husband, wife and son of 17 years. 17 nowadays is a man so the family room, the double and separate single ground floor with adjacent large bathroom would barely suit, but they wanted it. They booked, the price fixed for £25 each for a night. That was £ 75 x 3, £ 225. I said pay cash when you arrive as sending c/card details would be of no use as at this time I didn't have a machine to process it anyhow. OK came the reply we will see you in September.

They telephoned me and said they had arrived in England and they were hiring a car and travelling up to the North to see her mother and other relatives. OK, thanks for ringing see you next week.

The week went by and another phone call at 8 am came on the day of their arrival. All was well and they had travelled down and stayed in Oxford. They were leaving now and could make it here by 10.30 am. OK. She phoned at 10 again saying they were delayed and would make their way down to arrive at 2 pm now. OK, the room will be ready.

At ten to 2 the phone rang and she said they were delayed again and would not be arriving until 5 pm. OK see you then, then, then. Not mad about anything yet!

I waited in all day for this lot and so with a 3 hour window, off I went to do my shopping and other things. Being aware of the arrival time of 5 pm, I jumped in the car to return on time. It was 4.55 pm, precisely. My mobile rang and Bigfoot called to say my guests had arrived. I was less than 1 minute away at the roundabout, outside my B&B. I thought great timing!

Drawing up armed with shopping I entered through the side kitchen door to greet the family standing in the kitchen. "Hi!" I said, "How was your trip?" Then it started. The reply was terse from her, standing with hands firmly on hips with her back to the sink unit.

"We have been waiting 5 minutes now and you were not here to greet us!" I said "Sorry, you said you would be arriving at 5pm and it is just that now . . ." "I expected you to be here when I go to the trouble of letting you know when we are arriving!" Gritting my teeth I bit my tongue?

Trying to get past this I said well I am here now and can I offer you a cuppa. She said no thanks just show us the rooms and we can get unpacked. Rooms I said?

The father and 17 year old son had no words to say as yet, but the lovely young girl who accompanied them was a surprise to me as I thought that they had ordered, sorry booked a room for 3 not 4 persons? I inquired was all present wanting to stay? The reply, "Yes, can you give us another room, a double for us and a double for them?" Well this is a small B&B and I only had limited rooms available, 3 singles in the triple, or 3 in the family room. They discussed it and agreed that the mother, *hands on hips*, and the father wearing a *bright blue* fluffy jacket, would have the triple leaving the youngsters with the family room. Nice woman then giving up her double bed for the kids.

This was for 3 nights remember, so some price amendment was to be made. This wasn't discussed before they went to their respective rooms, on different floors. Hands on hips came down wanting to know where the wardrobe was in the triple room but as I explained this was not her room as she had given it up for the son and young girl. She said that the website had an apartment available and that would be more suitable. I told her that she had booked the family room at a discounted rate of £25 per person including the full Monty breakfast and the apartment would be available if booked at the rate of £100 per night excluding breakfast, as it had self-catering facilities. *I reminded her that it was her choice to book the family room by phone.* She was not happy, because she took for granted this apartment would be available. It wasn't tonight, but she could have it tomorrow if she liked? So, reluctantly hands on hips went back up stairs mumbling something about not unpacking if they were to be relocated tomorrow. The time went by with relative calm but I could not help feeling an atmosphere increasing, a tension in the air, a dark cloud descending.

I was making myself a drink as the lovely young girl tracked out of the bathroom, just across the hall from the kitchen only wearing a towel held up around her wet bits.

She spotted me making, came through and said she would like a cuppa as well and could I make one for her boyfriend, the son. I replied, "OK then, do you like sugar? Do you take milk"? Her answers were of little consequence as I was just happy to keep her talking in the hope that the towel she was holding might slip and show me a glimpse of something. All men think like this . . . . it's natural?

They went out for food and arrived back at 10 pm tired with the day's travel and all was calm. The morning brought the next instalment of misery. The young adults came through and asked where the dining room was and I told then that I had it temporary full of Yellow Rose's furniture bits and bobs and it was not available at this time so they had to eat in the kitchen, on the breakfast bar, with 3 high stools. Well three of them sat on the stools and 'bright blue', the father, sat on the stairs with just a mug of tea. Breakfast was served and to my surprise hands on hips said, "excellent breakfast" and I thought that the worm had turned, but no. The worm had only wriggled and after the compliment back she came with, "We can't stay here for another 2 nights and want to see the alternative accommodation". She wanted the apartment so after the other guests left we went up to see if the apartment was suitable. It wasn't as there were no wardrobes in there either. There were just beds, rails for hanging clothes, no wardrobes. The walk in wardrobe we had when I lived here with my family was converted to into another twin bedroom so . . . no wardrobes anywhere then. She said that this was not suitable and she said they had to leave.

She said she was used to a sea view at home. but as she was visiting her older son, living 2 miles inland around the corner from me, this option was out, well almost, as I said,' the apartment does have a view of the water works storage ponds'? She wasn't amused, so coming down the apartment staircase I said, "Why not try next door? They do B&B and she has rooms with wardrobes", said sarcastically. OK then, taking her next door, she went in and on returning said their rooms would be suitable, so they packed up and left. Wait a minute I thought, you haven't paid. Hands on hips said, "How much?" I replied, "£100 £25 each as booked". Bright blue spoke for the first time and said, "We are totally unhappy with this place and so I am going to pay you half £ 50". I agreed to just get them out of the door. They were gone, this cloud of misery, my misery, was lifted immediately. I didn't feel sorry for them next door. They were after all getting my dregs.

Only once before in my life did I really know what it felt when something was a blessed relief. The other time was when the saying 'bored to tears', happened when I was 8 years old, walking hand in hand with my mother up a high street to catch a bus home Mother stopped to talk to every other person on the high street and I felt I was 9 before we got to the bus. I was so bored to TEARS.

This woman, hands on hips, gave me the same feeling of total despair. I felt sorry for bright blue for a second until the realisation that he had ripped me off £50.

This would normally be the end of the story but no, same time next year she (Hip's), emailed and rang Yellow Rose and booked her family room for 3 days stay. Da-ja-vu ? She said to Yellow Rose that last year they stayed at another B&B and it was 'the worst B&B in the world'. What about that then, a world champion. They didn't even have a dining room to use. We had to eat on the stairs, terrible. *Yellow Rose said that hands on hips also commented that the place next door was no better, in fact worse. The rooms were small and compact and the place was run by an Indian woman with a creepy little man always hovering around, horrid, smelling of curry.*

She uttered to Yellow, "Our older son has a family home at the bottom of your road so your new B&B would suit us fine". Yellow Rose thought of my bad experience with her before, she thought of outback man, she thought of her Quad room with no wardrobe. She said to hands on hips the reason last year they could not have their breakfast in *my* dining room was because of *her* stored furniture, and so it might be a tad awkward to have you stay with me, just in case I did drop by to say, hello!

OK, Hip's has no option now as she has run out of B&B's around here. She can now travel 2 miles away and book in at the excellent 5 star beach front hotel with heated pool for only £85 per night each, without breakfast.

Then she will have the uninterrupted sea view she is used to at home. Lovely Jubbly!

I bet her son here loves the fact she only visits once a year, I know I do!

Chapter 23

The drive upgrade

I decided to revamp the front car park and drive. The cracked and tired concrete was an eyesore so as next door was going to have their drive 'done', I decided that I would get a quote from their contractors? I was in building and this type of work I could have done for myself, but I thought that it might not be worth my time getting all the equipment arranged that I needed to do the work.

The next door team arrived and so I went over and asked for a similar quote. The drive and car park was to have pea shingle laid in a black tar type liquid which hardened and held the pea shingle from migrating about. A sort of stone embedded finish. This I thought would be cheaper than tarmac and would look a sandy colour, better than plain black

Their foreman came over and measured up. "180 metres", he said in a strong Irish accent. "OK, I said, how much?" He answered, "Sir, I can give you a cheaper price as we are doing next door and all the stuff can be delivered on one lorry, saving money". "OK, I said, how much?" "Well Sir, you do know that we will spray the entire drive with our special base tar and this is quite expensive so yours will be a bit more than next door?" "Yes, OK, how much?" "You do have a larger drive than he does so the extra will be for that as well." "Right then how much?" "Yours will be £850 Sir, cash. No VAT." "That's £ 200 more than next door?" I said. "I know Sir, but yours is bigger and we do have to spray it all over?" "OK then do it—£850 cash, on completion."

I thought that as it is fixed with the tar spray then mine will be superior as I have a solid base to start with unlike next door's, on dirt.

The work started next door and the black barrel trailer and electronic sprayer was dropped off in my drive. The work progressed and they finished the neighbour's drive. It looked good and so they started mine. The drive was prepared by sweeping and spraying the concrete with weed killer. Then it was time for the tar to be sprayed on. I was asked to take my car of the drive for the day and leave it elsewhere whilst the work was completed. While I was gone they had completed the tar spraying and had completely laid all the pea shingle to completion. I was amazed at their progress and I must say first impressions did look good. I inspected the work and found up and above the damp course, and over the white door sill, a layer of black tar over spray. All up the glass of the white plastic door as well. I said, "Are you going to remove that?" and Irish said, "It will come off easy sir, with petrol but as I haven't got any petrol, can you do it?" "Well, Hell No?" I said, "You do it? Go and buy some over the garage! You can't leave it like that". He thought I was being a bit fussy. I was not pleased. Well off he went and said he would come back tomorrow to collect his money and would clean off the black then. He also wanted to leave his sprayer in my drive to collect at the same time. OK, the next morning he returned. He removed the black from the door and sill but forgot to do the rest. It had soaked into the stone plinth facings of the wall and was hard to remove. As his lorry was blocking the road and drive he was to be got rid of as soon as possible. I reluctantly gave him his money and he left. I had a receipt in my hand from a page torn out of a booklet marked with consecutive numbers and copy carbon, hand written. You know what I am going to say as the name on the copy was O'Reilly. Sean O'Rielly. There was a mobile number on it and I did ring him later. I will explain. After he had gone I kicked about a few stones and found the stones flying everywhere. I had paid for these to be locked into the tar that was all up my walls. Well I decided to clear a few away with my yard brush. What did I find? The smallest dribble of tar, trailed in a squiggle about the concrete with about 5 stones stuck to it and the rest loose. I phoned Sean O'Reilly and he said that his sprayer packed up after he had done the edges and all he could do was to drip from his bucket a small amount as he had run out of the tar and couldn't get any more. Even if he did he couldn't spray it as his machine was broken so he just laid the pea shingle and finished. I said, "Are you going to return to do it again?" "No", he said it would be too expensive for him to remove all the stones, spray it over and relay them. I would have to pay more money for that. He said he had under-estimated the amount of stones and he had to get another lorry to bring more as it was.

I gave up and left it like that. The reason I didn't get rough with him was whilst I was away my neighbour saw his men drinking cans of lager while in my back garden. As they spotted him they started walking back up my garden path looking everywhere as if they were casing the joint? I cannot be sure but 2 weeks later there was a break into my garage. Stolen . . . . 1/ road breaker, 1/ Petrol generator, 1/ Diamond petrol cutter, I/ compactor. Not stuff local lads would lift. Coincidence? What do you think?

I lived with this stone drive fiasco for a year and had enough. I bought some weed suppressing membrane, and laid it over the front lawn. I swept up all the stones and put them onto the membrane to form a base for my new arty farty pottery plant garden collection. I then edged all the perimeter of the drive with kerb setts and formed a drainage channel to the lowest point. I then laid block paving to the front drive to this drain and the rest was relayed over the old concrete with neat tarmac. I should have done this in the first place but to this day the only reminder of O'Rielly is the faintest of black overspray up the stone plinths. Have you **Seen** Sean O'Rielly anywhere? If you do, tell him to get lost, that's my tip!

Chapter 24

The 'CASSA' family!

These days some people who stay are welcome back any time. This family was no exception. They started coming years ago it seems that we are now talking to each other as extended family. The adult male is living in London with his new partner and her 2 children. The reason for his visits, on these regular occasions is to see his daughter, by a previous marriage. I have named them The Family 'CASSA'. It is their initials lumped together. I toyed with 'ASS-ca'. It didn't sound right, too much like 'ask er'! Or something rude,—like bottoms?

Only A and A stay on a regular visit but sometimes the whole CASSA family turn up for a night. This allows the children to get together, catch up and play outside their home environment. They have flying visits as both the parents work and despite half terms etc they have to get home.

This, in the main, is exciting for children as they go out to the beach and do fun things all day and can run around the apartment still excited when they get back. My only fear is that one of them might fall down the metal staircase leading to the garden, but mum's a good mother and keeps an eye on them. They still run up and down the stairs though and make the necessary metal rumble as they do. Their lounge is directly over my sitting area, and at night when one or more of them jumps up the ceiling fitting vibrates with a disturbing rattle. This I have been aware of for all occupants of the flat, not just the children. To be honest they are not as bad as the revellers. The 18 to 25 year olds are the ones that make most noise. They get a bit tipsy, play loud music and jump around before they go out at about 10 pm, when all goes quiet. I have had the slats under the beds broken on more than one occasion so I know they do a jig or some dance on the beds then either fall off, with a big thump, or jump off always it seems over the ceiling rose.

Recently we have been playing cards with S and C. He has a liking for a game called 'beating jack out of doors'. This game doesn't involve skill only luck and who ever ends, up with all the cards is the winner. I delight in teasing C by taunting the name Loser-Loser, when I or someone else wins. His face is a picture as he hates to lose. It make it all the more enjoyable for him to win when its 'payback time; He wins and taunts me with as much gusto and delight he can.

Sometimes I try to amuse the children with my silly tricks, when the parents are beautifying themselves in the bathrooms. I have string which I knot in a loop over one child's finger. I then hold my finger to theirs to complete a barrier that the loop cannot pass. I show them some tricky twisting moves of the string how to get the loop off. This looks impossible to them and I have fun showing them how to do it. There is a cork trick which needs agile hands, but my favourite is to get them to shout out the alphabet quickly. In fact I say, 'I bet you I can say the alphabet quicker than you'? Well as you all know children love to ramble off the ABC as quickly as they can at school, so a test then. 'I shout', 1-2-3 go! they start. ABCDEF . . . . I say ZYXWVUTSRQP . . . And they stop confused, Dot com? I continue unhurried to the end . . . ONMLKJIHGFEDCBA. I win nana-nana-nana? I learnt it like this.

Write it down backwards and sing it to yourself out loud as you are reading it. This makes learning it easier. Remember the first 11 letters, ZYXWV-UTSRQP. V and P rhyme. ONM_LKJ next, then IHGF, and finally EDCBA. The J and the A rhyme also. These help with rhythm and flow.

This some children learn and it keeps them occupied for a while. Stupid I know but there is a purpose. Try using your new skill to find your page in a telephone book. Go on flick through one and go to L or M? You will be lucky to stop on L maybe you stop on Q? Then in your head you recite the alphabet forwards to see where L is from Q.

I had to laugh when 'A' slunk off and went nosing about while we played more cards. She crept up the stairs and tried the doors to the other rooms in the B&B. She came running down like a scarred rabbit. I said "Where have you been?" But she didn't want to answer. I found out later that she had opened BIGFOOT'S bedroom door and he is a 6 foot 4 inch Yeti. She was looking up at this huge giant of a man, with his booming voice. (He's a bit deaf you see), asking her, "What do you want?" She just turned and ran back down the stairs with her tail between her legs. I didn't like to ask what he was dressed in as sometimes when I go up there, his doors ajar, He's sitting on his bed, playing with his laptop, just there in his underwear. You remember the tatty greys. Well maybe this is what 'A' saw, and that would frighten even me! It would frighten anyone as half an acre of white tummy fat bulging over his tatty pants is not a pretty sight!

Chapter 25

Block bookings and animals.

It is summer and this story involves a young friend who I met through his dad when doing some building work on his house. It was a shower room refurb and unusually a fish tank perched (excuse the pun), on a stone plinth my bricky built in his lounge, weird!

The friend ran a country and western shop, started by his dad who had the idea to take a back seat now the son was older. He was taking on his first large project. The venue was in a local large field. This involved a lot of organising and a lot of up front cash. The friend was on his own in this, as his dad thought it too risky a venture and that he was too long in the tooth to start this caper now.

"Other events like this are going on in other parts of the country", the boy said, "but have not been attempted here before".

On his Todd the friend told me of the groups he had already booked from all over, even one famous 'country' group from the USA. I went to see the site for my self as the event got nearer. This was quite an undertaking I thought seeing all the caravans, the tents, the dance floor in the marquee, complete with bar. There was a huge blow-up stage and the mass of lighting set out all over the grass. There were stalls being set up with all sorts of western wear, boots, dresses, tops, Indian head gear, you name it. There was even a fast on the draw tent with 6 guns firing blanks at an electronic target, registering reaction time. Hundredths of a second were recorded with the very fast guys, sorry, cowboy gunslingers. I saw a helipad and that was for rides up and around the ground for £40 a shot. Shot! Gunslingers!

It was most impressive and he said he wanted to book my entire B&B, for mate's rates, for the week. The group went up to the flat: the girl singer went in the single and various other performers in the rest. Number 2 was also seconded, so the bill for the week was quite high. He wanted to pay when he took the money on the gate on the first day, but I was worried that this type of gig could end up pear-shaped, so it was money up front mate! The cheque was cashed special clearance and to my surprise it went through, no problem. The accommodation was secured.

We had a free pass to the show and took our time, waiting for a fine day. On this day towards the end of the week we found perhaps 200 caravan and camper vans parked on site for the entire week's programme. These people took this as their annual holiday. I had no idea that this was so popular. We spent all day trolling around finding out about all the Westerners.

I found myself looking at the girls wearing high-heeled leather boots, sporting short colourful skirts trimmed with leather tassels. I think I was ogling. Don't see this down the high street every day, do you?

The event seemed to be a success but my friend told of disaster. The venue costs, the tents, toilets, security, huts, personnel, lights, generators, insurance. Everything cost a fortune and to break even he had to have 6000 plus people attend. He had, to date, just 3500 or so and this was the penultimate day. Rain and wind kept them away. Every one who did attend was well pleased with the setup. Great value they said. My friend was worried. He and his wife were broke and they couldn't afford to pay for all the equipment let alone the groups and other performers.

The bills kept coming and nobody was being paid.

The news got around and my friend had threats. They had to leave town to get away from his creditors. He couldn't take his loved parrot and asked if I would take him for good . . . OK! I was sorry for him and said I would take his pet parrot. Actually relieved, he gave me the bird including his cage, food and instructions for keeping the thing. The cage I rested in my lounge in full view of the dining room. I thought it might be a novelty. This parrot was beautiful white with a pink tinge to his feathers. Well this is how I saw him last year flying from his cage to my friend's wife's hand with elegant ease and with no fear. She could do anything to him, tickle his tummy, turn him upside down, kiss him and let him nibble her hair. They loved each other. He was most attracted to my bright turquoise ski jacket and at will nibbled off the little toggles quickly moving to the white zip pull.

They brought the bird round and dropped him off and said they both had to disappear for a while so please look after our parrot. Well it looked more like a stuffed sparrow.

All its plumage was nipped off. The bird had a habit of nipping out his new feathers as they grew nipped them out again. This was a disaster but not as bad as the next problem. He squawked with such a piercing screech that I had to cover him every time he did and leave the room.

I persevered with this for a week until I realised this bird was affecting my health. It had some sort of dust on its body and this was affecting my eyes, then my chest, I couldn't breathe and I started sneezing every time I went into the room.

He had to go!

I would lay him to rest in the garden grave along with the 3 Campbell ducks, that's how bad it was. These ducks belonged to my ex wife, bought for the children when they were young. They had a duck pond I constructed and then herself required a duck house with egg box. I obliged and for security covered all with wire netting. Lovely!

Their grave you ask, well remember our tame fox that sleeps on the camp bed in the greenhouse, he killed them.

Ex-wife used to let them out to run around the lawns sometimes. She was only away for a few minutes, but foxy had his way.

We used to eat the eggs from the 2 lady ducks that produced proficiently for a year until crafty fox put paid to that avenue of joy. They were slightly larger and slightly stronger that chickens eggs. When cooked held together nicely, fresh, lovely on toast.

So Isabella, Orthelia, and Casanova were going to have company.

My mate came round with his girlfriend—wife now—and he loved the bird, without his feathers, as he was, naked! She didn't take to him at all looking as bad as he did but he wanted him and they took him anyway. I got out the disinfectant, scrubbed the floor and plugged in the fanned ioniser to completely clean the house of the bird's death dust.

I sometimes see the parrot when I go around to theirs. I sneeze over him instantly. She still doesn't like the bird, he's drawn blood before and if allowed out he runs over the floor directly to her feet with the intention of biting off her toes. I guess he has not forgotten his earlier 'mum' who abandoned him. Living with me with no females about, he was just waiting for retribution on any female in his company. He chose *her* although they had in the house 2 grown up daughters.

Despite spending hundreds on Vets bills the problem still exists. His feathers have not been allowed to grow and he keeps nipping so he still looks like little more than a mouthful of meat. Don't parrot's live for 100 years or so?

Poor, suffering wife! The vet said he's a she. That explains it then . . . women?

I have to this day never heard of my parrot-giving friend or his wife but I hope they are OK and not ended up like the Campbell ducks? In a shallow grave

Chapter 26

The chicken bone

I had new neighbours and when they first came, were friendly enough. They are related to the original people that lived here before I arrived. Both my neighbours are now settling in doing their own work to bring their respective homes up to how they would like it. This one, in question we will call machine man. He was an engineer for his working life and was now retired. An early retirement was taken to allow in the new generation of young workforce. He then had his lump sum payment and was set up to do the alterations they would want. He was helpful to me even sharpening my blunt twist drills, a laborious job but one I was very grateful to have done. We had drinks and conversations in his new conservatory on many occasions. The common law wife and her sister were very nice and our relationship was cordial. I was invited to come round for dinner one night and afterwards to watch Shrek on their new large screen TV with cinema surround sound. This was good although the sound was too loud for me as I was deaf for about 3 days afterwards. Years of him being in a loud heavy engineering environment I suppose.

They had 3 little rats, sorry, dogs. They were wire-haired miniature terriers, tiny ones with bows in their hair. They warmed to me as time went by and even sat on the settee with me, and cuddled in while we talked. Nice. After a while they had an outside, 8 foot round water pool erected just behind the garage, on the lawn. This was in turn covered with one of those green and white plastic tents with the fly screen sides that they sell for

£99 discounted to £10 to clear. This kept the falling debris off the water and helping with the temperature. There was a slight humming noise coming from the water circulator but nothing annoying.

They wanted the leylandii trees adjoining our properties to grow above the permitted height so as not be overlooked by my B&B guests when the climbed or descended the spiral staircase to the flat.

I know why, as one early evening the three of them tripped, naked across the lawn to the pool.

Fun and splashing went on for some time and I left them to it.

This was acceptable but there was a problem brewing and it was the dogs. Every time I hung out washing, sat by my waterfall or on the garden seat, the dogs said "hello, hello!" again and again. By this I mean "yap-yap-yap". One started it and the other two joined in to help, and in the end a chorus of yapping. This I answered by shouting out "Dog pie", in a threatening voice. Not with bad intent you understand, but just to let them know it was me, their friend and sitting partner. This calmed them down and they went about their business without anymore yapping, unless I moved quickly or made a noise. This was getting a regular occurrence and in the end I asked the owners to try and keep them quiet. This was met with a blank stare. How? Why? We all love them? It's what dogs do?

We didn't talk for some time until I thought, was that the door bell I heard, and yes they both were standing in my porch, that is machine man and common law wife. Her sister was at work. Was this a peace offering as machine man was clutching an attractive bag? I invited them in and sat them in my conservatory, just off my lounge and made tea. I brought the tray in and we gathered around the coffee table and saw the attractive little bag sitting on the table. After a few sips of tea it happened. I was intrigued as to the contents of the bag as this was no doubt the reason for their unexpected visit.

His opening words were, "I have chicken bones in here". "Ah! Soup" I thought. "These were thrown out onto my drive, choking one of my dogs so severely that if I had not acted quickly she would have choked to death. I removed this one from her throat and the other bones were found on my drive, beneath your bedroom window!" A direct accusation! My mood changed and this was going to be the end of cordiality. She started to rant and I tried to calm down the situation. I asked "why would I or any of my guests throw a bag of chicken bones out of their window"? I provide bins for waste and anyhow it is expressly forbidden to consume food in the rooms as I only allow eating in the kitchen even if a guest has takeaway food. It could not have been me as my room is on the other side of the house. The only person that would be able to do this was Bigfoot. He, to my knowledge would not have the transport to get to Kentucky fried chicken as the nearest one is 2 miles away and he only has a second hand push bike with a wonky wheel. This attempt at humour was not going down well, so I changed tack. "What about seagulls?" I said. "They are always flying over here and often I find bones and stuff littered on my paths and patio". "Not this amount!" he said. I have got it. It's the fox. He must have picked up the bones and brought them through to you. I know he walks up my path, behind the conservatory wall, hops into your drive then pops out again at the front by my security light an onto the road. Sometimes this wakes me and looking out I have seen him. Perhaps it's him. Most likely! Solved?

They were not convinced and left without finishing their tea. To this day I still think they have a vendetta against me over this.

There was the time of my sons 16th and his band called something or other came round, can't quite remember the name, along with his school mates and their girlfriends. They all descended on the B&B, for this first time gig. A grand rendition of their music. Modern music that teenagers like to hear. He plays drums and with the children, sorry young adults, ready and waiting in anticipation the show began. This was a Sunday, early afternoon in October so the temperature was warm and I would expect the neighbours to be out, walking the dogs. The party started with an electronic guitar blast, a crescendo of drums and other instruments all joining in. All were having a good time. They came and got food and retreated to the bottom of the garden away from us older people. I noticed that they had made use of the old loungers the fox has adopted. We remained segregated on the top patio near the barbeque. Some drifted away as the afternoon went quiet, when one girl, scantily dressed for the occasion, shorts and top with belly piercing on show, came to me with an anguished face. "Someone is taking pictures of us through the hedge!" she said. "Where I asked?" "Down there, at the bottom!" she said. "I saw them but I think they have gone now." "Ok I will keep a look out."

Was this evidence gathering from the neighbours, to hand to some authority that I am making a noisy nuisance of myself, and was it justified? Did they think I was having this party on purpose to get back at them! Do they hate me for yelling "Dog pie" to the little ones? Who knows? Just that I suspect they are jealous of us having a good time.

In consequence, and surprisingly, I had a visit from the council asking me to stop my guests from throwing cigarette butts over their drive and investigating a further claim that I was running an illegitimate B&B? I was incensed. These people bought their house next to an established business, and knowing all that entails went ahead with the purchase and now they're complaining to the council . . . Right?

I have a strict no smoking policy anyhow as I detest smoking as you have previously read. I am thinking of taking up smoking again just to throw *my* butts over theirs!

The council officer's were completely satisfied with the arrangements I have here and went away saying a report will be in the post.

I wrote a very strong letter to my neighbours explaining that I do not want to receive any more complaints from them and if I do I will take legal steps to stop them. I sounded cross! I wrote about the dogs, the high trees getting out of hand and encroaching over my wall. The phone abuse from common law wife about the F—ing band noise, cheek! (She might have said *Rocking* but no. she didn't). Spying on the young girl party goer's by taking photographs of them through the hedge. (Can I have a copy?)

For me the final straw was them contacting the Council offices! Who else would have done that?

Since I sent my letter, all has been quiet and the dogs do behave themselves. At least I haven't heard them so much. We never talk or have anything to do with each other. Peace!

The trees are growing bigger and bigger though? Their may be trouble ahead?

Chapter 27

Digging up the new drive

Sod said that if it can go wrong, it will? He was right. It was a month after I had the drive re-done when a camera was put down the blocked sewer pipe . . . . under the new drive. I had the evidence that the 'plonkers' who laid the new sewer, fitted the connections with standard 4" clay sewer pipes. They did a good job making the falls correct and the joint sealed however the curved connections to drop into the flow of the main sewer were not so good. The camera found that the men had used straight pipes without curved sections. They laid straight pipes together and set the ends at an angle to turn it into the main sewer. This closed down the 4 inch round pipe into a 2 inch oval pipe and left rough groves used to hold concrete for sealing the pipes, exposed. This allowed the sediments in sewerage to build up in the grooves to cause a blockage. This was cleared 3 times in 6 weeks so something had to be done. The only option was to dig up the block paving and remake the drain pipes properly. In came the digger and digging 1.1/2 metres down lifted out some stinking slop dropping it all over the new tarmac, a hole that would swallow a car was excavated. This meant no toilet use for the day and night while the replacement pipes were fitted. The new pipes were covered with shingle, (don't start me about pea shingle), with concrete laid over the shingle to protect the pipes. The hole was filled in and compacted down and left to settle before the blocks were placed back into position. A jet washed off the mud and who would know that I was relieved of £1100 for the 2 day episode. It was back to exactly where it was before it happened. I was relieved that I could use the toilets again. I could just imagine what the guests were going to do, if they saw their toilets over flowing? Yuck! The drive was useable again and so with all this expense I thought I would trim the hedges and prune the palm trees to complete the job.

It's amazing that one thing leads to another? In the summer the trees have bunches of small white flowers. These need to be cut off every year as the spent bunches go woody and stifles the other leaves. The lower leaves go brown and fly off all over the drive. The clean up is necessary to make the front have 'kerb appeal'. I use large carpet trimming scissors to cut the tough lower leaves and generally tidy the tree. After this I get out the hedge trimmer and neaten up the leylandii, pruning the tops to gutter height. This gives me a pile of cuttings that needs a trailer to remove. 3 trips to the dump, crisp and clean. Just one more thing to complete the project was to install the front flood light to illuminate the car park, automatically. This will be ideal for the guests to load and unload.

It happened! As soon as you do something new! The next night a neighbour across the main dual carriageway complained with more annoyance than necessary saying to me he was being distracted from watching his television by my light coming on all the time. This is a man who has noisy barking dogs, every-time someone walks past his gate and has his headlights on full beam, right into my bedroom windows, as he leaves his drive at 5.45 am every weekday morning. On top of this he has, opposite his window, a pedestrian crossing with its beeping and coloured lights going all the time . . . . And he is telling me that *my* light is annoying him? He can get stuffed?

Chapter 28

The family from, Hell!

They booked to arrive on the Saturday, at about 6 30 pm for 2 nights. Their friends, who were staying just for the Sunday, would arrive early morning as they were starting out at 6 am to get here. They asked for a cot. Didn't have a cot so they said his would have to do. Handy!

They arrived, an overweight white South African lady with her English husband and the little one, asleep in his carry cot. I might have been a bit hard on her as the little one was only one or so, and she might still have baby plump.

The husband had a funny name like Royston David, and I didn't know what to call him? Dave or Roy anyway I ushered them up to the triple room as they said their friends were younger than them and they thought it might be best for them to have the double bed. Nice! They settled in and then it was just to heat up the baby's bottle and the odd cuppa that sent them off to sleep, early. In the morning their friends were to arrive soon after breakfast. It was 7 am, movement in the kitchen and on investigating found 2 grumpy faces shuffling around with a whingeing baby perched on the breakfast bar. I braced myself as they requested a change of room as this one was definitely not suitable. Apparently the baby woke early as the light through the Venetian slats was too bright, and he was used to having 'black out blinds', to keep him sleeping till about 9 am. "This allows us to have breakfast together in peace" she said. Well a special request I was unaware of until now, I thought. I said, "Let me see, you wanted the single bed option did you not?" "Yes, but we thought it would be darker, so can we have the double room back, as it will be quieter." The main road noise was also a problem it seemed.

After moving them to the ground floor room I served them an early breakfast I thought, if the window was ajar as the triple was, the trickling water from the pond might be another problem? Who cares? They were waiting for their friends to arrive and she went into the new bedroom to collect some seating device that was to be clamped to my £1200 dining room table. I was unaware of this as I was upstairs changing the sheets they had soiled last night, replacing them with clean ones. Coming down with the washing I found they had made themselves comfortable and static in the dining room. The baby was happily banging my stainless steel cutlery hard down onto my expensive dining table giggling all the while. I said can you please stop him from doing that as it is going to mark my table badly.

Unaware this was happening as they were both engrossed in the morning papers. Overweight lady reached over to baby and said, "Stop that!" and removed the cutlery out or range of his little mitt's to which he let out a horrendous high pitched scream as if they had been cut off. The damage was done. Roy or Dave looked up in annoyance at me for causing his boy to scream and said, "Look what you've done now. He will be upset for ages and we will get no further peace." I just walked away gritting my teeth and thinking who are these people. How dare they clamp some industrial device to my lovely table and how much damage has the little shit done?

He called me back in and demanded another pot of coffee and would I warm some milk for the baby to calm him down? Shut him up more like? Reluctantly I did and thought how I hope their friends will arrive soon so they will shove off to their Sunday do. Was this a religious meeting? Was I to turn the other cheek?

1 hour passed and the family of fun were still sitting in my dining room when at last their friends arrived. A cheery couple who had an easy trip down as Sunday mornings are usually quite quiet. I wondered what Roy / Dave would have made of the road noise if this was a weekday. Baby would have been up at 6.

Without a word I ushered them up to the triple saying this was the only room I had left but they were more than happy. They all went out and the rest of the day was mine.

Still clamped to the table was this industrial device with a baby seat affixed and I inspected the damage. About 20 to 30 dents were apparent on the otherwise mirror smooth table top. They are not getting away with it I vowed. They have to know this is not best behaviour and some responsibility has to be taken on their part. They came back and disappeared into their respective rooms. I still don't know the reason they came but an evening meal was arranged and they were soon out again. They were not back very late as I was still up but safely out of the way in my bedroom. I didn't want to face Roy / Dave or his fat lady so left this delight to the morning. There were noises in the kitchen and this was I suspect 'fat' lady preparing the warm milk. The second couple didn't want breakfast so they left to get back but the funny family wanted the full Monty again. I chirped up and said, "Would you like a large pot of coffee this morning Dave?" He replied, "Yes", with a quizzical look. "It's just that you asked for more coffee yesterday and I thought it was not enough. Is there any special request for this morning's breakfast?" "No, just as it was yesterday thanks." The room was silent and the breakfast was rustled up as quickly as I could. I wanted no delay in sending them on their way.

No hanging around drinking coffee and no little brat to make more marks. The meal went without a hitch and I said if you would like to retire to your room I will repair, sorry remake, the table for today's evening gathering. We are having a séance tonight. I lied to get them to move. It worked and they retreated to the family room. The baby had his milk and the thing he was sitting in was removed leaving deep indentations under the table.

I just wanted them to go and it seemed an age before they did. The shower was constantly being used and the comings and going across the hall with wet feet, interfering with my routine.

They eventually left but not without one parting gesture that got my goat.

His car, a big 4x4 thing with the usual family crap on board. This included sun block mesh on the side windows, to keep the baby's eyes safe. A baby on board sticker plastered over the rear window. On the back seat was a baby cot thing with all the nappies bags and colourful toys. Dirty paintwork!

This monstrosity of a vehicle was parked angled across the drive, straight in from the road with its nose parked nearly in the front entrance porch. Nobody else could park properly. The other couple squeezed in the corner having to reverse out onto the main road because other later arriving vehicles had to line up tight against the hedge.

Well I had to say something. I asked when baby was in harness and fat wife was just loading her double sized suitcase in the boot along with all the baby accessories. "Did you have a nice stay?" I said sarcastically. The reply was "Yes, very nice thank you". "Well I'm very happy you did. Please don't bother coming here again as I found you the most irritating couple I have ever had stay. You are ignorant and have no regard for anyone other than your selfish selves. I have a damaged table, loads of cleaning up to do, not to mention the fiasco of the room changing? You contributed just £60 a day. I don't think it was worth it for all the hassle you brought. By the way just park where ever you like! Anywhere will do.

They left also having to reverse in a multi—point manoeuvre. They're gone! Good riddance, the relief!

Every time I polish the table these dents bring this episode back to me. It's not good for my demeanour?

Chapter 29

Some-thing, Nice

This couple came every year. This was the place they loved, not particularly my B&B but the area. I called them George and Mildred after some TV show that I never saw but heard about. I thought it apt. They had a healthy appetite as every morning they came through to dine on the full Monty breakfast. Mildred would have her routine and was boss. George just went along with her for the easy life.

We talked about them living in London and how her brother was nearby so they would visit him to catch up. Every day lunch was at a local nationwide chain of fish and chip shops. This one, on the coast, was George's favourite. They had age on their side and as this place did pensioner's specials, this was something to do with their full chubby look, not fat, but happy.

Every day was full as they didn't arrive back until at least 8 pm. On arriving home I always brought them a cuppa. Its' hard work sightseeing! This went down well as I made sure that I had a piece of cake for them to eat. I varied this from day to day so I think they liked guessing which cake was on for tonight. One night I said, "Come home early as I have somewhere I would like to take you". They came back at 5.30 as asked and they plumped down in my baggy old harlequin settee, remember the ones I gave to shed man? Although old, these were comfy. The only problem was I had to lift them out of the settee if they wanted to get up. Mildred said that staying here was like living at home. I wonder who lifts them out at home then?

They wanted to know what was in store and I told them, "Wait and see?" I knew that in her younger days Mildred was a fan of a local team event near where she lived, and as there was one near here I thought, as a treat I would invite them to go tonight.

It started at 7.30 pm so we had time. I said get ready for a night of nostalgia. They both looked in amazement as to what I had in mind. I didn't let on, yet! I said to get ready and wear some warm clothes. It was August but the nights still get nippy sitting around. Oh! Nearly gave them a clue.

I had the tickets and off we went. Unknown to them I put 3 cushions in the boot of George's car. He was driving as this was familiar for him, and I sat by him with Mildred in the back. We drove some 3 miles and arrived at the venue. It was alive with cars, cars parked every where but I knew a place and we got parked easily. This was it, Mildred's first time at a speedway meeting since she was a girl, and 'Boy George', when they first met, all those years ago. George could not believe it. I had the cushions and bought a programme to write down the results. I even had a clip board for Mildred. We got seated on the hard wooden grandstand bench, cushions under our bums, and the racing began. We were sitting right in front of the starting gate, the noise of the engines as the riders revved up their engines. An ear shattering noise reverberated around the covered stand area. The smell of Castrol 'R'—is better than a £100 bottle of perfume to a speedway fan. It's like nectar to the nose. The dirt flew back as the knobbly tyres ripped grooves into the shale track and the race was on. Thrills and spills were not disappointing. They raced in fury and the home team won this first race. Mildred wrote down the results from the excited commentator loudly announcing the time and the finishing positions of the 4 riders. 5/1then.

This is very satisfying for the home team but we didn't want a runaway victory as that would be non-competitive. Each team has a star rider and these guys are international standard so on any track they are hard to beat, even for the star home rider. Team riding comes into play as the points system is 3 for 1st, 2 for 2nd and 1 point for 3rd. now't for last.

As the racing got to half time I went and got refreshments for as all. We were ready for the second Half. The programme Mildred was clutching was nearly full of results and as we arrived at the last team race the scores were level. This meant that a 3/3 would bring a ride off as it would tie the meeting, a 4/2 or 5/1 to them would have the away win, and for us it was sudden death, a must win situation. We had to finish first and third at the very least. Our pride was on the line. It was on a knife edge. The 4 best riders of the night would line up for this last race. The engines revved and the tapes went up, an even start. The first to the corner was our man; the second was yes, just . . . his team mate. A roar of approval from the crowd was deafening. We had the proffered start positions 1 and 3 on the line as we had won the coin toss for this last race. Our star rider hit the front on the first bend, and had to nurse around his second string team mate therefore keeping the opposition from overtaking. The race continued with the threat from the away team, constantly worrying the number 2 seed. 2nd lap, 3rd lap, and the big push for the points brought home the winners. A 5/1. We had won and the stadium erupted with shouts of joy, the horns blasting out approval for the home team. We were on to win the league this year and this just cemented our position at the top.

There was a second half and the short break for the individual riders to collect points that they would add to their nights tally. More points meant more pay.

We were calming down and I could see the old folks had had enough. It was a long day. We left the stadium early and got to the car unhindered as the rush for the exit didn't happen until later. George asked, "Do you want a drink in the local pub?" I was happy to go home but Mildred said, "OK, just one".

We stopped on the way at a pub I know was good. I wanted to have comfortable seating in a nice atmosphere, George bought me half of cider and Mildred had the same, George had water and a bag of crisps.

We talked of the evening and Mildred said that was one of the best nights she ever had! I was pleased. She remembered all the sights and sounds this night brought back. She looked satisfied in her own thoughts. We finished our drinks and left for home. I said goodnight and saw them in the morning as usual. They left for home a day or two later but booked for next year. A tentative date, to be confirmed later. Mildred did phone in March the next year and confirmed the same room and dates as before. They never came. This was not like her and I wanted to know why. I didn't even have their phone number. George paid directly into my bank the fee for staying and didn't want a receipt. I never used call back or registered their number. So how could I get in touch? It wasn't long ago this happened and yesterday, a phone call from Mildred's brother. "Cancer!" he said, "Both of them". George diagnosed first then Mildred.

They both had died within 3 months of each other! I shivered.

Chapter 30

The very odd couple!

These 2 arrived on the doorstep from a phone booking the week before. They sounded nice on the phone as Yellow recalled. They came by Coach to the town and public transport to the B&B.

These 2 were odd.

I did not have direct contact only observing from a distance when I called to see Yellow. They were in the garden, sitting on the 'children's swing' that Yellow had kept from the old owners. They were puffing away on fags. That will please her I thought?

She had to report that they came down for breakfast and these 2 were, well, not suited. He was a brute of a man, short and stocky; sporting what looked like a cravat under his chin. On closer inspection this was a massive tattoo of flames licking up around his throat. She was a picture of beauty . . . Not. She was Scragg as Yellow called her. She had full makeup on and wore what she considered a good outfit. It consisted of tight pants with skimpy top showing her skinny midriff, high heel black shoes, worn down heels, you know, scratched up. She had black dyed hair, thick with hair spray. Not a pretty sight.

She was not sure why these 2 had come down here but she did know they drank. It was the first night and they came in late, rolling drunk and loud. Yellow was born in London and these 2 were from her neck of the woods also. Only difference was they came from south of the Thames. It was the way they talked, in a sort of 'ello', and 'all-white' slang, with an apples and pairs London accent. Soon the noise stopped and they slept.

The first breakfast was cold as they took an age to smoke their fags before coming in from the garden to eat. No doubt the last night revelry was taking its toll. Smokers and drinkers don't usually want breakfast. Yellow rose didn't like this as she had the breakfast hot and ready and was kept waiting for 20 minutes for them to finish smoking and you know her feelings on smoking.

Eventually coming in and pushing the breakfast around the plates they said they were off to the beach. A day of sunshine and, no doubt, booze. She was dressed in the same clothes as she arrived but he had changed into a black tee shirt and jeans. The tattoos were evident on his arms as well as his neck in the tee shirt It was revealed that she was 5 months pregnant at her age of 40. This was her second child as she was married before with a 20 year old son. This time she was having a child with the tattooed man. It turned out he was only 24, himself. This is a mess waiting to happen?

They were out for the rest of the day and came back early on this their last night. Apparently they had enough of the healthy seaside air and got a bus back to have dinner at the local pub. No noise tonight and in the morning they went through the same routine as yesterday morning. This time Yellow waited for them to finish smoking and started the brekkie when they sat down. After breakfast they packed up and were ready to go. They asked if their suitcases could be left in the hall as they would go shopping this morning and come back later to pick them up. Their bus would not go until 6 pm, so they had all day to shop. He arrived back at 5 pm and asked for the cases. Yellow Rose went to see where she was but he was alone. Asking where she was he said, "Waiting at the bus stop, right!" He had to rush so he made his escape as swift as possible only to say what a lovely time they both had and they definitely would be coming back'. Not on your Nellie, Yellow thought. No way! She didn't want to say anything as he was a big rough tough guy and she thought he could turn nasty, so she just let him go without comment.

The facts are these 2 managed to leave their room in such a state it was no wonder the woman would not face Yellow to say goodbye. The reason was the bedroom was completely covered in makeup. The beds, the sheets, the wall, the cushions on the chair, even the pillow had an eyelash shaped mascara mark on it.

The bathroom looked a little better except on investigating the neatly laid out towel on the rack, Rose turned over to reveal, yup! You've guessed it—a big black make up smear mixed with blusher.

On top of this they didn't have a pub meal, they had a takeaway curry. This was dropped on the floor and although picked up, the stain was embedded into the carpet. The bed was moved over a bit to cover it up. The curry boxes were chucked in the bin by the bed. They might have even had the curry the night they came home drunk? Anyway it was a mess! When I asked, "will you have them back?" Guess what she said. "Are you mad No way".

Chapter 31

The old man!

When Yellow Rose came to live here she was amused over the way I talked about some of my guests. Every one I gave a stage name that was memorable. This was variable depending on how nice or nasty they were. She constantly heard me talking of some by a generic name. I used this because my guests, in question were not known to her. The generic name was 'Scrote'. It sort of rolled of the tongue. She asked what was did 'Scrote stand for? Well traditionally around here the generic name for a holiday maker was 'Grockle'. I don't exactly know how this word came up but being by the sea side I expect a good guess would be a derivitive of Cockle? It might even been a typo error C to G, who knows? The words, Scrote and Grockle are not found in any dictionary. I definitely know where my made up words come from as I made them up. Scrote is a shortened form of scrotum. I decided that this would be a good name because it is slightly derisory, and adequately describe the nature of the guests as they mostly leave the towels, bedding, and tableware in a wrinkled mess. Not unlike a scrotum?

Some comic said that God must have had a strange sense of humour as when he made scrota he used some left over elbow skin!

So Yellow Rose now calls her guest's Scrote's, as like me we are the ones who have to clear up their wrinkled mess.

The old man then? He was nearly seventy five and was proud to tell Yellow his age. He looked a bit fragile and pale but as the name describes his full on wrinkled skin fitted into the Scrote category perfectly. I thought he did fancy her somewhat and would have liked to take things further than just landlady and guest. Well good for him I thought! At his age and still wanting romance?

He had just finished renting his house abroad and was looking to buy a flat or small house in the area to be near his ex-wife and daughter.

I believe the old man is very alone. He had a jerky retiring presence around others. He was independent though even as it was clear he wanted some body to be with. If this is the case what could be done?

I would not encourage Yellow to help but as you know, she would if asked. Was old man asking? It was a strange affair as after old man had breakfast he would go out, come back in, go out again and back in? What was his game? All this back and forth, for what reason? He didn't smoke, he was just . . . being busy.

Yellow had him scheduled to stay for some weeks and over this time you would think that he would get to know and trust her. He always asked, as he was staying for a while, if he was going to get a discount on his B&B bill? It put yellow in a poor position balancing his 'amour' against the money he was to pay. She had my policy of, NPNS?

No pay no stay, yet in the old man's case he didn't want to pay as he went along, weekly in advance, as was the norm. He wanted to pay at the end. Well 2 weeks went by and she insisted. You have to pay me for your keep, now. This was an affront to him. He didn't like that as he would have no power over her! He went upstairs to get the money and never came back down with it, he just forgot. Was this his game? Was the old man a control freak? I tried to find out. I tested him. I asked, "Did your wife live with you. Abroad?" "She came to visit now and then. Actually we are divorced, and since the divorce we have become firm friends again." A big statement!

Was this the reason for his skittishness? He saw her and his daughter on lots of occasions and things just jogged along. Perhaps he wanted to rekindle the marriage? He had found a place some 7 miles away and it was time for him to go. On the last day I went round at breakfast time. Their breakfast was a lazy 9 am. Mine was done and dusted by 8.30, so up the road I went, to see Yellow and see the old man off. I had not got to the bottom of his antics but just as I resigned him to being an enigma it happened. He said that he was always distracted from being happy as he always had in his mind a clear vision of how things were going to be. Marriage, children, all was in its place until the tragic accident?

"My son was killed outright in a motorcycle accident some years back and I can't ever get it out of my head. I can't get over the fact that I have lost him. He was my life and he is gone forever!" He trembled! Was this the cause for the marriage to breakup?

I was full of remorse for not giving him any grace for I knew nothing of the old man before he arrived and only wanted to know what made him tick. I hope he finds peace soon.

He did pay as promised. Yellow took a chance and got the full amount owing at the end of his stay. All in all we both felt that we should show some more compassion with our guest's fragile nature, but when do you . . . knowing all that has gone on before?

Chapter 32

The American accountant

This guy was big and had a funny gait. This was because he was tossed off his push bike on his home street in America. He was an accountant and he lived in the USA with his wife and grown up children He had a sister living just out the back of my B&B. He wanted to rent a room for a month. He wanted to have full on internet connection which was handy as I had just upgraded Rose's internet service the week before. She was used to having a computer but didn't feel the need to go online as she used mine. I gave her my daughter's old lap top and organised the connection through a wireless server. All was set up for her guests to use the system by entering her password. This was the first mistake I made as the word I used was her personal password that she wanted to be kept a secret. It goes on but suffice to say I changed this to something innocuous and all was serene again.

'Cycle man' was installed in the upstairs single and it was soon apparent he didn't like the little room. He was moved to the quad room and beds were moved so he could spread his wings. He had 2 laptops and a host of electrical gadgets, printers, scanners, chargers, you name it. This was a complete office setup so a different rate was established for his new 'penthouse suite'.

At this time Cycle man had a big car to transport his stuff around but was giving this up as he didn't have to go far to visit his sister everyday. He was going to work at home and he could walk, or should I say limp up the road to her's for dinner every night. This was a bit too far for his scarred and battered leg so I rented him a bike. This was an off roader push bike previously on 'loan' to my ex-cleaning lady who was to give me £25 for it. She never did! All the time she was cleaning for me she borrowed it and when she left she locked in her shed. Well I wanted it back so I recovered it one day and this is the machine I hired out to Cycle man!

He had set up his computers to work on his accountancy for clients all over the world. He had just come from Bahrain or Saudi, the middle-east somewhere and was visiting his sister en-route to America. He was on a one month working holiday.

He couldn't get connected through our wireless system as it was not enabled yet, so Yellow took him over the road to get a dongle. This was a tempting name to call him as he bought 2 dongles, one for each laptop, running simultaneously. Just think 'Dongle man 2', Sounds like a sequel?

I was busy with building our new conservatory when 'dongle', sorry 'cycle' man arrived. As he was an academic this building work unfolding in front of him held a fascination for him. He would stand and look at progress every day. The erection was swift. I had the frames up on day one, and the box gutters in place on day two. There was one problem when Cycle said to Yellow Rose that the noise I was making fitting the conservatory was disturbing him. This was of no consequence to me as I was 'progressing' the job and Yellow wanted this to happen. She was after all in her back bedroom sharing a loo with everyone who stayed.

The reason I was building this was to enable Yellow to have her own purpose-built annex away from the Scrote's. I was going to remove a side window, adjacent to the kitchen side window and door, from her bedroom wall to make it into a doorway to the outside. This doorway would go directly to the car park so building a conservatory on this side of the house incorporating the adjacent kitchen window and door meant she could walk through and access the kitchen as well. Effectively this would allow her direct access to her bedroom through the conservatory. Building works didn't end there as now Yellow wanted to complete the operation by getting me building a double sided wardrobe with a walk in shower/wc. This, involved blocking up the bedroom door to the hall, now redundant and facing it with a cupboard and on the opposite wall a similar cupboard, and between these the shower/wc. The plan worked and an en-suite bedroom was constructed. The noise then was offset by Cycle making his, 'own' noise. At night the road was quiet and you could hear a pin drop so when he revved up his laptop the printing and general moving about was just as disturbing for others, sleeping. He would sometimes work into the early morning as American time was 8 hours or so after us. This was when his phone calls and exchange of data were made and sent. The American's were up over there, so 50/50 noise then? Get stuffed Cycle, grin and bear it like we do!

Cycle came down every day to see progress and asked me what I was doing with this roll of blue cable, sticking it to the floor with gaffer tape, in a single geometric design. He really knew nothing as this was the under floor heating cable fitted before the latex floor screed was skimmed over to form the base for the travertine marble tiling.

This tiling was to make more noise than he could muster with his lap tops as I was about to embark on tile cutting.

The machine arrived from the hire shop. It was a massive beast of a thing, taller than me, with wheels and a water tray to collect the cuttings. The first cut was a try out to see if the machine was cutting square, and it was. It cut through the marble like a knife through butter. Noisy, wet, very wet, creamy white splashes all up my clothes and over the new planted trees. Yellow went mad so covers for me and the trees not to mention the new tarmac drive were sought. All day this noise went on but Cycle man was resolved to it by now. He was delighted in the result he saw. Something of which he would never do or I suspect would never want to.

The job was coming on and the entire time Cycle was here he was a party to the culmination of Yellow's household comforts.

I do feel a bit guilty though as the internet *was* up and running the day after Cycle arrived, but I didn't let on as I didn't want Yellow to be charged for reams of downloaded Data that he was generating. Dongles saved the day. There was one thing I was relieved about from Cycle, and that was he gave my bike back to without any damage. I didn't bother to take out accident insurance for him knowing he is a risk having had an incident in the past. One other thing? He gave me his paper shredder, how nice? It's at my feet under the computer desk, as I write this. Cycle was a nice man to have stay

Chapter 33

The trainer!

She arrived with her brightly coloured outfit sporting a large overnight bag. A spritely blonde with a sunny personality! From the car she wanted to make sure that her belongings were going to be safe and I assured her they would be, as we had video surveillance cameras about the place. On signing in she had a cuppa and we talked about her job. She wanted to tell me she was a nurse but this was not the entire story. She was, in fact, a trainer of nurses. She had been a nurse in the past but was elevated to training as new procedures were ongoing within the NHS. She said she had expensive equipment in her car so her inquiry was valid. We finished tea and she gave me her credit card for swiping through my machine. The business done she asked, "Is there any place to eat?" Just as it happens a new pub/restaurant, over the road, had opened a few days before and I had some free discount tickets she could use. I thought that this would be a good way to check out the 'new brooms' over there and ask her, if she didn't have food poisoning in the morning, what the food was like. I like to go to places on recommendations. It was about 8 pm now and she was off to the restaurant. At the door she asked again if her stuff would be alright left in the car over night. I was concerned that this stuff was so expensive that it might be better stored indoors. I asked what was so valuable. She opened up the back and brought out a huge metal case. This was plonked onto the floor when she started to explain that this was a training aid for nurses. This was made especially for the action and technique training for the insertion of drugs. Well I was about to be trained, here on the floor of my car park. I looked around cautiously as we were in full view of anybody watching. The floodlights had come on so we were illuminated good and proper. Then to my horror she produced a life sized flesh coloured torso of a human body, a lady's body. Well it didn't have any hair on it so I assumed it was a lady's. This torso looked just like a bum from the back complete with holes in the places you would expect them to be. It felt squidgy, unusually life like. She took the bum firmly under her arm and showed me her finger.

Her finger had a well manicured nail, coated with bright red nail polish glinting in the floodlights. I dreaded to think what she was going to do next. She put her finger onto the crease of the bum and with definite force pushed her finger right up and into the tight little hole. "Ouch!" I thought. Was this a tad unusual for me to be experiencing this with a youngish woman I had just met? "That's the way we do it now when it is deemed the best route!" Right I said!

To be honest I have had this procedure myself when I was admitted to a hospital some years back. I have had a suppository gently inserted by a lovely young nurse. It would have been a better experience if I was not in so much pain. I had a kidney stone for a week, not nice. I recall that the lovely nurse was on shift only for that afternoon so with my luck a rather large male nurse took over from her. He was the night nurse and it was him who had the job of re-drugging me. Well he came mincing over and introduced himself. I couldn't help noticing how big his hands were in fact I thought they were bunches of bananas under the plastic medical gloves! Without asking if I had any experience of taking drugs this way he proceeded to insert a new, what I thought was a double sized, suppository on the end of the biggest finger I have ever seen, right up my jacksey. Not nice. It's amazing how the intense pain quickly goes away when drug taking time comes around.

2 other guests came out to their car. They were off out to dinner as well and I wondered if they would want breakfast tomorrow seeing what I getting up too this night. They saw me watching this girl with her finger up a bum, showing the push technique to me. She asked, "would I like a try"? I declined trying to show no embarrassment. I quickly said to her, "I think that your 'stuff', (another pun), should be safe in the car over-night". I didn't want Yellow Rose coming round and spotting this large rubber bum lying on my dining room table. That would be too hard to explain away without a glass or two of vino, and without bum girl to 'back me up', (there I go again with the puns).

In the morning our nurse came through to the kitchen for breakfast and sneezed. I asked if she would like to try my local honey on toast. She accepted. And then I said how about trying some honey tea I had. This was supposed to be good for allergies. I said how was the meal last night at the new restaurant? "Great she said". I might have to go over there myself sometime with Yellow as a treat. I asked her if she was single and she said that her long suffering husband was at home with their children. I wondered if she practiced on, him? No, don't be filthy! It's breakfast time.

Despite this I did like Bum girl. When she left after breakfast she said she would return to stay again. I shook her by the hand with only a tentative grip, remembering where it had been the night before. I thought now she was gone and I could get back to normal by explaining to my other guests that she was a nurse and it was ok as she was only showing me some technique . . . but not yet. This episode was not over. I was serving them breakfast and I heard a noise coming from her bedroom. I went to investigate and there it was, her mobile phone stuffed down between the bed and the wall, perched on the wooden edge of the mattress base. She had a call and I answered. It was her husband wanting to know where she was. Well I said at work. He asked why I had her phone and it sounded a weak excuse when I replied, "Your wife has left it here, by mistake!" He was not convinced. I said I would return it to her if I can find out where she was working. He didn't know so after my other guests had left I walked over to the local industrial estate and made some inquiries. Searching around I found the NHS department for training and fiscal studies. This building had a reception with a well dressed assistant, asking if she could be of help. I said I was looking for a nurse training meeting that I hoped was here. The nurse trainer had left her mobile phone at my B&B. I wanted to give it back to her. She made a call and within 2 minutes out from the 'bowels' (excuse me! puns, can't stop) of the building came our bum girl. Well she was delighted to see me and on receiving her phone back, kissed me full on the lips, gave me a hug and thanked me profusely. All I can say is at least she didn't shake me by the hand. She will be back and I can't wait to see what I am going to be trained to do next.

Chapter 34

The Motorbike man

It's funny how people influence you some times. I had this guy come and stay for 5 weeks or so. We were on the same plain as we both liked motorbikes. He came in his car but as we talked he wanted to bring his bike down so he could use it in his spare time. After staying here for 2 weeks he took the train home and returned on Sunday with his Honda 750 V twin. The bike was black which is rare as Honda only made the black version for 1 year. He was obviously it proudly as '*she*' did gleam in the afternoon sun. This made me envious as I had only a year or so before sold my Yamaha 750 Virago. Our winters and other reasons combined made me reluctantly, sell. His arrival had my interest in bikes perk up all over again, so I asked if I could have a go. I had a Honda 1000 before the Virago and I knew what to expect with performance etc. Off I went togged up in my old leathers. The bike handled good and the performance was, for an old bike, up there. Just one problem I found was the gear changing was not so smooth and the handling was a bit tight. I came back and said nothing about it. I didn't want to upset him. "Lovely, thanks for that, what a machine! I do miss the thrill of acceleration and top speed. It's balanced just right." You have to remember this is an old bike looking nearly new, in showroom condition. He had work done on it for the MOT. It had the steering bearings and this might be the cause of the stiff handling. I left him to go to dinner. We talked further and it was decided that he would take me pillion to a local bike rally. We arrived on time and perused the bikes on show. We looked at a Virago, its chrome bars and exhaust pipes, glinting like diamonds in the low evening sun, with the beautiful metallic green tank shouting at me, "Buy! Buy! Buy! Well the price was what I got for my old Virago so I thought, "What the hell, I will." I offered the guy a reduced amount and he thought about it. He said no. We left and returned later in the evening.

I asked, "Was the bike sold yet?" He said no. "Will you take my earlier offer then?" This time he accepted and I was to be the proud owner of a Virago again. We went home and Bike said, "You lucky sod! I loved that bike as much as you and if you hadn't bought it, I would have." That evening I told Yellow Rose what I had done and to my surprise she didn't mind too much. A couple day's later with bike man at work we drove in my car to pick *her* up. The day was hot and sunny and we were quite excited. The bike was washed and polished to perfection and parked 'ready to go' outside the bloke's garage. I had my first ride up the country lanes just to make sure *she* was working well. I've had much experience with this style of machine before so I knew what to expect. The gear change and the shaft drive were smooth and the bike handled like it should. On returning from my test ride Yellow Rose and I sat in his garden while his wife brought out the tea and cakes. We chatted about why he was selling and it turned out they needed the cash for a building project. I didn't ask as I have finished with building. I released from my pocket a bulge of £20 notes and counted them out in front of the wife. She was the accountant here and after confirming the amount was correct I duly received the documents along with the receipt for the cash bundle. The deal was done. We said our goodbye's and left quickly just in case the bloke started crying about loosing his bike. Well it's a man thing.

Yellow took my car and followed me riding home on my new shiny green steed. Yellow said she liked the bike as this one had a high backed chrome leather 'sissy seat' for her to sit, secure on pillion. We did go everywhere on it and bike man was very envious. Yellow Rose cut a good figure on the bike with long yellow hair flowing back as we rode. He saw this and thought that *his* girlfriend would have liked this ride. He had to have it now. He kept on asking if I ever wanted to sell, he would buy.

Well we rode out on summer evenings and sometimes he said if I wanted we could swop bikes. So we did. He was hooked even more now because although the 2 bikes had the same size engines, his was racing-sports and mine was . . . Cruising!

His job here lasted longer than he thought as they lumped onto him another project so Bike man extended his stay only going back home sometimes at the weekend. We became mates I think as we would banter with each other which only comes with familiarity. Some people commented that we were 'too close', my new best mate, but that never crossed my mind, only theirs. You remember the pink jumper episode? I was offering to clean his bike and had some special stuff that brought the white painted alloy wheels up like new. Perhaps this was what they were talking about as they never got me to do anything *nice* thing for them?

I had by now told him about the gear changing problem. It wasn't him being a bad rider it was rough because of the wear on the chain, and sprockets. I organised them replaced at my local bike repair shop and at the same time I had them adjust the steering to let it run smoothly. It did the trick and now his bike was as smooth as a baby's bum. It had to be tested. I roared up the dual carriageway and had all the heads turning. What a noise, the roar of the exhaust, beautiful raw power, a delight, a nuisance to some!

One weekend he had taken his car home for clothes and papers were too cumbersome on the bike. He said if we wanted we could take the bike for a spin while he was away. We did one Saturday. We went for a day trip around the countryside and ended up some 30 miles down the road.

I liked his bike but Yellow Rose was perched up high on pillion and she had to hang on to me for grim death. We stopped for lunch and hoped the weather would keep fine. It did but on the way back I found that holding the handle bars of a racer was tiring on my forearms, especially when braking hard when Yellow Rose slid into my back. She put extra pressure on my arms and I was getting fatigued. I tried to get her to brace herself on the petrol tank when braking but she said my tummy was too large for her to get here little arms around. Right, a good excuse! Too much lunch maybe? This was the only thing I disliked about his bike. I must be getting old or fat . . . or both?

Bike man was going home, his job finished. I genuinely found myself thinking I would miss him. He was gone and so was his bike and car.

I did sell my 'new' Virago to him a month or so later as promised. Now we call him 2 bike man.

I have a little scooter to Take Yellow Rose out on now and then when the weather if fine and warm. I have to use 4 wheels for long trips and carrying stuff but when 2 wheels gets into yer blood its there forever. I have to say I have been thinking of a Trike! One of Yellow's guests has one? Forget it she said. 2 Bike man and I still keep in touch.

Lightning Source UK Ltd.
Milton Keynes UK
UKHW040633071021
391760UK00013B/61

9 781450 079044